FAT ART, THIN ART

FAT ART,

THIN ART

Eve Kosofsky Sedgwick

Duke University Press   Durham and London 1994

© 1994 Duke University Press

All rights reserved

Printed in the United States of America on acid-free paper.

Library of Congress Cataloging-in-Publication Data

appear on the last printed page of this book.

Selections from *The Warm Decembers* appeared in *Raritan* 6.2, Fall, 1986.

"Sestina Lente" first appeared in *Massachusetts Review* 25.4, Winter, 1984.

"Trace at 46" first appeared in *Diacritics* 10.1, March 1980.

"Sexual Hum" first appeared in *Salmagundi*, Winter 1979.

"An Essay on the Picture Plane" first appeared in *Poetry Miscellany* 5, 1975.

All are reprinted by permission.

Contents

I

1

Who fed this muse?
Colicky, premature,
not easy to supply, nor fun to love:
who powdered her behind and gave her food
the years when ("still a child herself almost")
her mother was too blue?

  "Almost"—I *was* a child.
Blue, I was blue; even more I was green.
They mystified me too,
the red protuberant
organs hypertrophied with self-abuse
from which we thought back then
a muse like this emerged.

Her grandmother was willing, so I kept her,
lucky I could so choose.
My family fed this muse.

And it was in a suburb she was schooled,
like me, among assimilated Jews
in the American creed
that nothing could be very different from this
or much better. It could be much worse.
On TV she would watch the Museketeers.
At a parent-teacher conference, Mrs. Tarrant,
her fourth grade teacher, told me I didn't
"know what a treasure I had there" in her
which wounded me; who'd say such things for *me*?
And I minded that she went
so ardently to Mrs. Grove and Mrs. Wittman
and her friends Julie, Nancy, Don, Meganne, and Susy
and *their* moms, who she thought were wonder-moms.
For two years, I swear, she wouldn't let me
cook for her. I'd beg. She would refuse.

She acted like she thought I'd poison her—
that was the start of her terrifying revulsions.
(It's true, cooking was hard for me.)
And I, I always had to thank
the teachers and the friends who fed my muse.

I have to still; I want to.
Is there another story, a better story,
than the young muse in search of nurture, and finding it?

Today they'd call it an eating disorder
but I never heard of such another.
Greedier than a dog,
big-boned, rangy she grew up; was sometimes gaunt,
then fat—and those fat times
it was like somebody who hated her had tied
clumps of upholstery stuffing all around her frame.
The flesh fell off her just that easily, too. As if
she never quite digested
the things she ate—
not in the sense of storing them as muscle or as fat,
in some shape that would be her own shape;
say, she had no reserve.
It frightened me (I had my own "weight problem").
Her belly like a wineskin:
round, sometimes, as a kittenful of milk,
then the same day
slack like in a dustbowl photograph.
It meant that every person, all her life, who ever
stinted this muse one crumb
threatened (they didn't know it) her survival.

And every single hand that ever fed her, saved her life.

(Iciest of questions for a muse:
Is there any more where that came from?)

Of course, I was *in love* with her, a lot,
we were so close in age; but in the way of love
maybe it wasn't something she could use:
my eyes that dwelt then in her face;
the rhythm of my day
molded to her furies, her despondencies,
the gaiety of her, her way of switching
always ahead of me in her ragged right margin—
so I could never pay attention to *my* work.
Even today I've got nothing you'd call
"work habits," though I've worked so hard.
By the time she was 12
I was cemented to my muse's moods.
Maybe you'd say she didn't have a self?

But she would court me too!
There was this gruff, butch thing she'd do
like she was taking care of me in a scary world
that I ate up—who wouldn't?
                                    Did I know
how all this grim sublimity
in the tight-budded, clumsy ingenue
could have been called as easily
depression as (what she would call it) speaking true?
Enough to worry: *that*, yes, I did know.
Worry, the only gift we always gave each other freely.

After that suburb, everything was news:
there we'd been used to always being used
to everything we saw. Not pleasure, okay,
but pleasantness, and plenty, a cautious plenty
we thought we could assume
—lucky we: almost imagined the world could—
and heterosexuals out the wazoo.
(Except at scout camp; what that place had been

for generations of baby lesbians
it was for her. And I, as well, was happy there.)

Later, after she'd run away from me
all those times I would wonder
sometimes how much her grueling aptitude
for silence and aversion
owed, maybe, to the domestic politics
of postwar—when the thing you asked your courage
would be, How to refuse?
How to go limp when you're hailed by the Law
in the shape of a state trooper with a dog;
to leave, like the Unfriendly Ten,
the names unnamed, to test your eloquence
in untestifying to the Committee.
A song my muse would like to sing
was, We shall not, we shall not be moved.
Except—another thing—she couldn't sing.

And with her bad feet, never learned to dance
through years and years of the lessons she liked
for the sociability, for all the pain. . . .
She thought—and later our friend Hal would say it to her—
it was in her nature as she was born
to be elastic, even graceful; she somewhere had
a voice to sing that was mobile
and affecting, and she wouldn't (of herself) have knocked
things over all the time or jerked so much
from the strange deadness to the strange
propulsions; somewhere *could* carry a tune.
Which she both liked, and found it painful, to believe.
Because, then, what had happened?
What was the spell that bound her throat and feet?
Tampered was a word she often used,
with (implied) a point of interrogation trailing after.

Questions I couldn't answer,
story I can't tell. Even probably I don't know it,
like the story of her leaving me;
of all the times she left, and stayed away; let *her*
tell, she's the muse. (If she will.) The plainest fact:

for years, while she was homeless, I was housed.

Was nourished, and gave nurture. Had my own
queer enough aesthetic, it turned out.
Had even my own loves, which weren't all hers.
Fat amazon, found courage, such as it was,
including if I had to
the courage to survive her. Learned more about the shape
my own refusals took:
never to claim. Never to disavow.

And did she, those years, toil, and did she spin?
Whose was the sanctuary that took her in?
Supply that kept her synapses synapping,
maybe it was the care she always had with her
from friends we'd shared, or hadn't,
the old loves—old attention—dear praises from of old—
dearest of all, severity, sobrieties—
the chaste, and sometimes the delirious, things.
        Some friends to me unknown.
Many I know so well that even now
they are "our" dear ones.
Some dead; some are estranged.
Many, even, I now fear that I've forgotten.

This morning somehow she was at my side again—
it seemed so natural,
an "I" I guess I am when she is there.
(But maybe not the old one; maybe an "I" that fed
as much on the longing for her,

on the body of her long refusal
to be with me.) She beckoned, she
enfolded me; enfolded me with her.
She took the coffee cup out of my hands.
I fell into it all,
the vat of her unmakings, her returns,
bottomless eyes, her halting narrow tongue,
all the old saturnine
ways whose only hint
of the utopian is how she reckons
that somewhere in the making there are souls
she'll teach the skills of hearing her
silent No to the last
loamy and bitter reverberation.
Her presence seemed a promise to me, and I was happy.

            *   *   *

So (Proust says), telling the truth
in our book
we lie in the dedication; but this one is no lie.

Only she and not I
(but here she is) as best she can,
gracelessly even, if graceless be her way
can proffer both our gratitude to those
beloved, who fed this muse.

Joy. He's himself today! He knows me!

No good outcomes with this disease
but good days, yes—that's the unit
for now, the day: good day, bad day.
From under the shadow
you wield this power to
be (or some days not to be) yourself,
to recognize and treat me as
(or some days not to), as *my*self.

Thus, to make me myself
by being recognizable to me;
not to unmake us both,
turning away,
joining your sullen new friends.

Grave, never offering back the face of my dear,
abey: let me take some more pictures
from this dramatic low angle by the footstool,
pictures I won't be in,
his face homing toward mine.
Catch him mugging with his pretty sisters
(one cuts her eyes drolly away,
clearing a place to be sad)

—and wait, please,
for the 1-Hr. Prints, then let me assemble
a big pseudo-David Hockney photo collage;
also hold on till I'm old enough to go instead,
even just tag along.

Guys who were 35 last year are 70 this year
with lank hair and enlarged livers,
and jaw hinges more legible than Braille.
A killing velocity—seen another way, though,
they've ambled into the eerily slow-mo
extermination camp the city sidewalks are.

In 1980, if someone had prophesied
this rack of temporalities could come to us,
their "knowledge" would have seemed pure hate;
it would have seemed so, and have been so.
It still is so.
        Yet every morning
we have to gape the jaws of our unbelief
or belief, to knowing it.

The Navajo Rug

I wouldn't say that, delirious,
he's "not himself." Eye-dazzler
left to ruin on a loom
the weaver was forced to abandon,
he is here in the unfielded, blinding
patches of what's been himself,
and if you knew him, you can see it all.
The bolt of his graciousness
like lightning with no sky;
his fury, his very own fury—it is nonsense;
the dry, thrown storm of his ravishing sentence.

Rug that's still on the loom:
a writer, just turned 32.

A Vigil

Gary, have you ever heard of a deity,
maybe a Hindu one, who's an elephant?
I think he's blue. Who's a god of love
or trickster, turns up all over the place,
named, maybe, Ganesh?

Fever makes Gary formal.
"I believe that is correct." Then he resumes
exploring with his stuck-out tongue
the inside surfaces
of a bottle-green, hieratic snout
snapped on for oxygen
over his own, lovely snout,
ashen right now.

Because you know you look like that
(with the long large-bore, corrugated azure
transparent nozzle out
from the more than semitically noble green
muzzle of the thing
under the all-night ICU lights).
                              —That proboscis!
Also the new dances I see you
doing with your hands, so graceful,
so imperious, I'm never sure
whether you're inviting a hand to hold
(I hold one hand with him already) or
banishing some subject (me?) eternally
from your countenance.

(Or feinting at a gallantry
to distract me from
his unattenuable intent of plucking out
the insult of some tube—some needle.)

Gracious comes the response, but lethal.
"Must there be so much speech?"

Later I'm almost asleep in my chair
and Gary's fluid-swollen lids are dropping
over his green mask
and his magical blue trunk, and the dance
of the hands begins again
so elegant, and he specifies,
"Inimitable.
The dance is inimitable
because it is so refined
and it is going on at every level, all the time."

The Use of Being Fat

I used to have a superstition that
there was this use to being fat:
no one I loved could come to harm
enfolded in my touch—
that lot of me would blot it up,
the rattling chill, night sweat or terror.

I've learned that I was wrong.
Held, even held
they withdraw to the secret
scenes of their unmaking.
                        But then I think
it is true they *turn away* inside.
It feels so like refusal
maybe still there is something to my superstition.

For years it drove me crazy
your funny pudeur,
the way you would refer to "your condition"—
If he can't even say the words,
I thought,
then how on earth's he ever going to . . . .

                                        Well, *what?*

What vengeful predicate
waited under my tongue?

"Your funny pudeur"—but today I cling
to my little phrase for you; think it
invokes the cheap and dear
indignity of the living
in "having traits."

Performative (Toronto)

"Does it feel to *you* like we're saying goodbye?"
"Are you crazy?"

                           But we were trying;
we hugged each other, and for a while we cried
because my car was waiting in the dark
morning, and Michael had decided now
was time for him to die.
The touching made us feel absurdly vital;
when we were done boo-hooing we just giggled.
"Is this what's called denial?"
"Oh, honey, denial's gotten us this far."

A honk in the snow outside.
—Oh, and he did say he liked my work,
he wanted me to keep on doing it.

Performative (San Francisco)

It is the long moment of no more
Goodbye in our vocabulary.
You take care—I love you—Be back soon.
Only not the shaved disyllable,
humble as dust and vengeful as a god.

The ancient story of any pedestrian
who thinking nothing of it
plucks just one modest flower
beside a modest road
—one snap of waxy stem
and from it flooding out, unstanchable,
the clotted gouts of blood and blood.

The horror in the taxi.

What I would be when I grew up,
I never wondered that (maybe I knew that);
I wondered other things: if I'd be
sane. Loved.

                    But I did
bend to divine one thing,
the fate of—"my talent." Shyly
as a big sister I would yearn
to trace its avocations, its vocations,
what *it* would want to be when *it*
grew up; what it would need the world to be.
Say I've abused, betrayed it a thousand times:
still I am grateful
there was even that bad way to care for the child.

Not like the clownish, friendly way you talk
with the big asthmatic laugh,
breaking the rules from shrink school,
answering all the questions
like, "Am I more this way than other people?"
"Do you think this *nicht mehr leben*
groundnote of a life can go away?" "No,
probably not." No, how I wish to write
is like you listen. Grave,
never offering back the face of my emotion,
only, the face of you listening,
it sinking in,
the violet in your thick cheeks.

Sh

He's not even Jewish, and mispronounces
folie à deux; I had to conclude he wasn't gay
when I came in one day
boiling, and bounced into my corner
of the sofa, and "fasten your seatbelt," I announced,
"it's going to be a bumpy. . . ."

                              "Fasten your seatbelt,"
he mused, "wonder where that metaphor
comes from?"

                  Can't fall in love with how a word
gets knotted with the saying of it;

finds my SM fantasies "abstract."
But say it's Jarrell I need.
He reaches to the bookcase,
he has it, *The Lost World*.

I can tune my mind today
to the story I think I want to tell you,
I can tune my eye
already to your face, listening.

I see now that this is the rain of today,
which will rain all afternoon; I'll probably
still have the same clothes on
when I breathe that same, little waiting room smell
of Main Street Clinical Associates.

I know that smell by now; I'll recognize it.

Yet it's the thing I can't, in advance,
tune up my nostril toward:
That's the way you'll surprise me.

"All I know is I woke up thinking,
better tell Sh about 'all this
suicidal ideation.'

No idea what *that* was about."

Snap-to-attention:
that's how I think of it,
the next thing that happens.

At a big auction, wagging of hands
to get into the bidding,
but then—the dip of an eyelid's
plenty for meaning.

          And so, it seems
I want your steeliest beam.
Regardless whether of love or mistrust.

Snapsh

That smirk! Maybe he's self-consciously
trying to look more intellectual, or slimmer,
or froze at my black mask and flashbulb eye.
    I think it's his anxiety to hurl
across my crises and the week of his vacation
a care that I can use.

Of course I'm glad to have it.
His grizzled nappy halo, downcurved eyes, and a glimpse,
grandmotherly, of powdery upper arm.

Why won't the proffer of such comforts
comfort me?
Why mask out, at each viewing, with my hand
the smooth, huge foreshortening of his own?

Crushed. Dilapidated.
Then come the truest sessions
of sweet Sh thought.
I've never felt so close.

It's also why I love
after a near tornado
the yard, the mud, the morning
in their new, punished clothes.

The 58 1/2 Minute Hour

Kind and characteristic ways to do it.
Oh no, we need to stop. Or,
what do you think—a good stopping place here?
Or with a groan, another awful place to end!
Even, if it's a too awful place,
the wave permissive: no; no, finish.
(Sometimes I even think it's both our protest—
No! what you want to say, I want to hear.)

Then comes my task of making it less mean,
the show of voluntarity, the cheer,
as my ten skilled, obedient fingers button on
a childish raiment of alacrity
and up I have to stand, and go.

How Not to Be There

The imposing woman with a tiny, feminine
presence—she's found one way to go AWOL.

Another way's the silent mantra.
"I wish I were dead" is a good example.

The silvery, insinuating voice
soaring free from the body of depletion
or repletion, is good when folks are fighting,
also in rooms full of love and interest.

Do remember to palliate all blame;
also, if you have a grave disease,
to be preoccupied about your health.

Not to be there when trouble calls your name.
Not to be there when anyone is ashamed.

Mobility, speech, sight,
a bowel, a genital, a hand to grasp,
a feature of a face, I'd hate to lose
those, but—a breast; a breast is *nothing*
comparatively.

                    I've said this so much
to myself, that I sometimes need reminding
it is *something*. Or was;

                              it must have been,
so must its loss have been—
yet I am so impressed
with my skill at zoning it out!

                    Maybe
I'm lying waiting for some other, little surgery,
and it comes back to me,
smothering me in lymph and tears.

A scar, just a scar;
I saw then
how I would get to know the oncology nurses,
when I was going to faint
—and she was only needing to get some blood—
and with her small severity we crossed the corridor
to rows of curtained beds and whispering,
her insistent with the needle, someone's soft tears
and a far murmur that only barely
wasn't my imagination, "spread your legs,"

hearing which I knew
someday soon I'd feel more nostalgia for this
than for any school I'd been to.

When I got so sick it never occurred to me
the cause was not your hating eyes.

A friend told me a year afterward
you asked about my health.

Then in my thoughts how willingly
I entertained them all!
—the ordinary things that might cause illness.

Little kid at the airport practicing
her tapdance steps, gazing through her bangs
and visibly trying not to be seen to think

There's no proper audience for me here.

No one will marvel at her, pick her out
and "discover" her, etc.

                              But, who knows?
Anyone really might, despite appearances.
So *don't* look gauche or (worst) self-conscious.

Of course I identify with her. Also with
the 3-year-old sister who (embarrassing)
clumsy from servitude
mimes every move she makes,

no trace of self-consciousness,
no audience consciousness,
simply because her big sister is making them.

In dreams they're interchangeable — my husband,
my big sister; I'm with someone to make us
and waking, can't remember which.

As if

the furrows of my path to her
wore almost to the quick,
as the eye's ear from syllable to line
staggers its numb, repeated drag
of the foot, mauled and mauling, that still though numb feels pain
across the never again to be resistances
to meter — in that rereading where the "by heart"
dull impulse of memory first speaks its part.

The only touch today, it seems,
the breath of my desire can make on Nina's, is
through her shy windows now licked from within,
the joining of their gaze toward some other form of life.

Our

'Night, Lovely dinner! Thank you, 'Night!
Aproned for ten minutes in porch light

what's any front door but the two-way-facing
stage set for its single, specialized

inveterate drama, titled "Exeunt,"
the one where actual marriages are performed.

They go inside to tidy up, to bed,
discussing us, and you. We go

to our car discussing you, and them.
While you—brown eyes opaque as scare-quotes

go to your own car thinking what you think.
That's a part of marriage too, our marriage:

all the precious perceptual residue.
Your envy, your revulsion—

Nothing fails to be turned to (our) account.

It seems there are two kinds of marriage;
it seems each has its one permitted grammar.
The utterance from Happy Marriage has to turn
into mood: the Pharisaic mood:
the imperative. Uncandid and unlovely.
And almost as bad is Unhappy Marriage,
its sliced, abject person of revelation.

The coed on her honeymoon
preregistered for "George Eliot and Flaubert"
reading *Daniel Deronda* in the frail airplane;
learning to be pleased and to please,
the silent corridors of marital exemption—

Always, I wanted marriage inside out.

One of us falls asleep on the other's shoulder.
An hour later when we peel apart:
in the fat of the shoulder, artful, improbable
brand, the double outside curve,
an ear.
For hours (shower, clothes) it doesn't fade.

How much mourning there already is,
warm and elastic membrane, between us.
The girl of 19 who doesn't bear thinking about,
for instance; the patience of her young husband,
the inexperience and violence,
the patience succeeding on patience,
married nights of no, no resistance—

That depressed girl: how inexhaustible
the motive she provides!

Not

I didn't put in for a transfer to this planet,
I can assure you. I *did* assure
my parents of this over and over
when I was a kid, which endeared me tenderly
to them. I'm sure.

It was the most raucous, outraged thing
I owned: the wish not to be
with its coarse baby sarcasms I treasured,
not to be and not to reproduce.

Did I imagine with the perfect
sneer or shrug that I could buy
myself the privilege of looking
sad? Duh. Like I would.

Nicht Mehr Leben

                 At eighteen
her old life abandoned her
in swaddling clothes that were
painfully worn—almost as painfully clean—
on the doorstep of her new life.
Where, yes, there was abundance
and only not enough small creatures to use it all
and always, always the kindest eyes
for her.
              It was strange,
they found later she didn't understand the language
the note was in—in someone's spiky script
pinned to her blanket. It was the only clue.
What she had to hold on to, and follow.

I'm safe so long as the single feather of one wing
trails its tip in the river, slow, deep, cold,
of real sadness. I don't ask for Lethe then,
only the drip in the quiet; the ache; and the scrabbling
rudder of tailfeathers to dip or dive.

Because, no, what's fearful is the long, granular lid
of freezing mist a yard above the surface, and to flog
with sodden icy wings
through all that blinding atmosphere of "grim" or "cheerful"
preoccupation—through the bucketing relay—and through
disfiguration of the id and mind and flesh

all the way up high to where, it's said, I may
someday rejoin my kind.

In dreams on which decades of marriage haven't
laid a paw the ordinary, fitfully
talented girl in my writing class
raises her ordinary freckled eyes
to me confiding a sentence
of which I lose, in translation, everything
but the one phrase—"My father,
I mean my Master—".
A stain that's spreading too fast for the blotter.
The way the upthrown lashes of
this child entangle with, or tease, the long
fringe of her bangs! It's like starting a book,
the way your fate and preoccupations,
hundreds of things, the allergenic roses
in the garden where you've thrown yourself
to read, flirt with what seem the thousand tendrils, all
responsiveness, of those
knowing solicitous first paragraphs,
as if another fate—

                         as if what you may be about
to read, the all of it, may itself be about—

In every language the loveliest question
is, You can say that?

Trace at 46

I.

In middle age his bodily outline
softens and fills in—partly, he supposes,
with femaleness. Brooding over himself
in his mother's bathroom, this strange month
of her illness, gives him pause, and also pleasure.
These adipose breasts, these accreting hips!
Besides, his new way to spend hours of days
—naked on the toilet, his thighs crossed, the penis
that now except in full erection always feels
vestigial, pressed out of sight between them—
lets him write, daydream, or do something
that feels like both. Letters to his wife, to
different women—"Sweetie," he starts indeterminate,
and then just writes. Distant cities
(and, nearby, his mother's hospital)
seem full of women who may be his, or him.
Distant, they sprout (he thinks) *in* this gravid
body. All that spacing feels like heaven.

March in Chevy Chase. His curvy abdomen.
Several times a walk through the house, or out
in the raw garden, ends in the same way
with Trace too uneasy, growing tired
of the excitement that does not decompose.
Nor will it, in nostalgia, disgust, or something
more involving, quite engage
the rooms around him, the pale and round
upholstered pieces, the buoyancy that unmoors
and floats them here from the rooms he grew up in.
Why can't he work on getting the current chapter written,
on Fauré? Dressed or undressed
throughout the house, "sweetie, my gut

leads me like a pearly side of salmon
rolled through a restaurant before the soufflé"
to the wet window, to the fridge whose
impersonal but responsive brightness opens
on his mother's favorite foods and his — yogurt
and eggs, rice pudding, cottage cheese, whatever's white,
easy to swallow, given to spoilage;
or soon to the piano. On the wall behind it
a landscape of his mother's. Some passages of melon
into an icy lavender
remind him of Derain, and the collapse
among them of the picture's rhythm, as if
a dancer or a typist should over
and over be unable to perform
one single gesture, a porte de bras in mid-turn,
or typed again "invisibele" for "invisibly"
wrenches him with impatience, not so much
at the mother neutralized, for the moment, in
a narrow bed, as at the passage through himself
so innocuously of the courses of arousal
leaving, as in the Venice of Fauré, sous l'eau qui vire
le roulis sourd des cailloux, no word, or note.
With mixed feelings he whispers a new phrase,
I am the track of many conveyances.

2.

In the bathroom, he's writing "to" the women
an odd memoir, his own? that, or nobody's.
"Late one night, in my fifth year, my parents
came to an unsurprising decision,
to separate. Then the glass lamp on the night table
was switched off. They touched hands across the space
and turned in their twin beds, and quietly
invited sleep, meaning to hold off
any devastation till each was alone.

Between them they had money—this apartment
was a large-roomed one in the east 60s
so, as their eyes grew used to the darkness, broad
milky-lighted boudoir space streamed in
over them, washed by the venetians.
They couldn't keep their eyes shut. My mother,
I know her insomnia so well, threw
an arm over her eyes. My father imagined
a thin rope with knots spaced out along it
pulling through his fingers as he counted
knots. That worked. My mother took a pill.
Spaces of potential mourning and
excitement, these two struggling to keep
and to relinquish control, worn out, were asleep
an hour or two later. When the door
opened.

      Drag, the drag of feet, of breath taken,
a pull of bedclothes, woke them. In the instant
of lunging separately toward waking, the interval
in which the new, decided-upon separation
came whole to memory, each one imagined this
or something like this: that the little boy, that
I, had somehow within sleep divined
how violence to the small world was going on
somewhere, and had been drawn awake
or sleepwalking, an animal magnet, to
this room, where the magnet's presence and gravity
might with some new imperativeness not
let them part. The breath in the room coarsened
in the instant that my parents leapt in relief
and resentment toward consciousness, toward me.
Everywhere, catching in darkness
the breath coarsened and moved—
a voicelessness that grew, second by
second, so extensive that it emptied

itself (to the waking pair) suddenly
of the meaning, 'little Trace.' More like
a pregnant, abraded west
wind drawn through the unconsciousness
that clung in the boudoir, a wind that urgency
or repleteness roughened. A moment more
prolonged

        Just as, in some affairs of the heart,
there are two languages, each made of the waste
or excess matter—the structure—of the other
and the two languages are silence, and speech,
and each language has only one meaning,
as, speech means love—silence means no love;
so that our transactions of each week, my addresses
to you, with the silence that breeds, points, and spends them,
   which they
gorged with their one, colorable meaning
deny and impoverish—turn abruptly
each week, at some quiet instant
like other quiet instants, in your ears
to intricate corrosive refusal of
love: speech laced with silence turning
to silence pivotally laced with speech:
the small machinery gearing just one more
quantitative plus in-
to the blankly, gaggingly different,
      Now in this bedroom the machine was ready.
One circuit of consciousness commanded the room.
Slewed by one least, hoarse, rubbled,
incremental breath, the presence flicked
into intelligibility; stayed fast. With that intelligence
the scattered pair was awake, because
legible in the drag through milky night
was the despoiled path of resisted pain: was adult pain

of an adult without a voice.
The third adult in our house was the au pair.

   (And now *I'm* scattered. Part of me, lines back,
addressed to you, is still wrestled
between refusal and love; and some part scuds ahead
plying across the fitful or sustained currents of narration
and gusty, then transparent, with relief as the distance from you
widens and clears.)

                  Homesick for Manila,
only eighteen or so, this girl must have worn
from the first meeting at the airport some
sullen, contracted blazon of overachievement:
the overseas-edition *Reader's Digest*
in her hand, say, and the one deep fold
pressed vertically into the vellum forehead
of the impassive, very developed face.
Tonight she scrabbled without a voice,
the oriental girl whose voice before had come
accented and veiled out of the rangy body.
Always around her I imagine or remember
was an atmosphere of overplus, like a kind of perfume
that heightens then extinguishes. Maybe
her heavy personal weather never
shifted, or even thinned, never
precipitated, until the night she moved
through my parents' bedroom: tearing
with pain, with no voice, with a
new blazon: a white stain around her mouth.

   In the kitchen, two things were discoverable.
An almost-empty steel saucepan had been
upset, and left an ineradicable
dribble. A half-full can of 'Red
Devil' lye crystals sat on the table.
How firmly she'd put her lips to the heavy rim
and with what patience and impatience she'd parted them

for long draughts from the up-tilted pan.
'Eat me, and I'll eat you' was the legend
the can might have worn."

3.
Everyone in Chevy Chase goes to shop
at Friendship Heights, at the Saks Fifth Avenue.
From two intersecting flows on the first floor
into the almost stirless bays upstairs
slip waves on wavelets of consumption and expense
past things that anyone with eyes would desire, past
some unfortunate, weird lapses, past visible
outcroppings of the underlying stuff, the handsome,
unindividuable wovens these women
cover themselves with every day
—this year, often in desaturated beige,
a lovely champagne—past these
and other things, injecting dreamily
into the drift of everything within these walls
a substance, money, like a kind of dye
that traces and opaques the tide of energy
and inattention (tide may be floaty but
knows where to go), like the luminous streak
of radium or barium the body gulps along
some unaccustomed channel, that on the X-ray—

Doctor, how did I get to "X-ray"? Wake up now.
All right then, let's see.

Even for habitual shoppers, moving through
a big, opulent department store involves
a complicated setting-in-motion
of charges, anxieties, pleasures, needs.
In Trace, who doesn't often shop like this
and who's been lately so much cooped up alone,
the sheer amount of stimulus, and its tonal

monotony, and, outside, the afternoon
closing down to early dusk
start belated trains, variously freighted,
of thought and muffled desire. Walking
over, he's slipped into a corner box
an envelope addressed to one of the women
with the account in it of the suicide
of the au pair in 1936. There
it sits. Trace at Saks wants to assemble
things for women, for different reasons:
for Dana, an anniversary present
(twentieth), for Flo, in Paris, turning 47
just ahead of him, maybe for his mother?,
for Cissy, since he can't be in Chicago
to see her conduct "Aquarelle" at its
première — golden embassies
or hostages, he thinks, spent into women's lives
and held in them estranged. At Costume Jewelry
silk cords, thick and thin ones, in blues and greens
for necklaces, have loosely knotted to them
exiguous silver leaves. Rainy strings of silver
that coral branches punctuate; pallid
satin ribbons, three or four crumpled together
through the fingers of a tiny furled silver
fist; folded money-purses in dry pouchy kid
on their own metallic-filing-colored
neck ribbons — all dangling glosses
on a kind of dressing not quite
imagined, but glimpsed as an exigent
rinsing glamor one impossible inch to
the side from real art. From Fauré, say,
whose walky bass lines, with their vagrancy
and thoughtfulness, one note for each beat
even in the most Venetian, silky
writing, are on the point of occasioning

for Trace—himself, as a writer, hesitant and circling—
a group of direct, ambitious sentences for the chapter;
direct in proportion to the distance, and not just
geographical, but also made of mistrust and anger,
between him and the human objects of his desire.
Walking through the decor, and pausing here and there
to focus or buy, buying one thing, a thin envelope
of gold metal, on a gold neck chain, with a flap
intricately hinged to disclose a wafer-thin
gold card that can slip out: "I love you,"
the blank gold envelope less than 1″ square—
from his *bouffée* of relief in buying
and pocketing the thing, from how joyously intense
his faith is in its power
to mute and assuage, he judges also the countervailing
magnetism of 90° north
fury and plain reproach, that pastes
into their distant orbits the huge clouded characters of
his present firmament. And in the high houses
of the astrological sky, as in the remembered
or imagined pale flat beach houses by which
he figures to himself his own life, and those of people
he knows, the animated passages come
from somewhere behind. Behind the opaque
almost unbroken frieze of flat houses, by
which really he denotes marriages, move, he thinks,
their color sucked out by the beachy brightness
of the day, and again eaten up
in the failure of the light at dusk,
transfusions of summer people so magnified in scale
that the cells of their lymph swarm in the dry air
like penscratches: a narrow constellated tide raking
a chalk-faced *plage*.

        Trace thinks he has in common
with other happily-married offspring of broken

marriages, a near-heroic pathos about *intactness*
of the home, as if the fragility of homes
were hereditary; really, he feels that he wasn't himself
during his own childhood, that sullen
or abandoned moments alike only blinded
him to his own efficient function
as the cover—addressed without ambiguity, later readdressed,
then crossed and then recrossed—for unforgiving things
his parents meant each other to know. The abrasions
of marriage, and there are some, he and Dana
are quiet about at home; vivid thing he tells her
about private unhappiness centering on his
almost fetishistic ambitions for the Debussy-
and-Fauré book, get hidden from the teenagers
with an odd zeal; and finally, his relations with
other women, substantial though they are in resentment
and bondage and imaginative nurturance,
seem when he thinks of them at *home* so thin
and ejectible, that his complete silence about
them to Dana feels, at some such moments, guiltless,
and accurate. His father's style of sexual misbehavior
in the service of prying that family apart
and keeping them, through little Trace, well-fixed
at a strange distance, he repudiates
so intently, with a repudiation
and a silence so badly undermined.
And speaking of silence.
                        One of the ways
he's trying to recuperate for himself
the death of the au pair is a second narrative,
an unspoken one that imagines an obsessed affair
between his father and the girl. The strains
of discretion that would have imposed! And how
much better at it than his father, any foreign
adolescent, who would, like Cissy, *froncer le sourcil*

and hold her tongue after whatever obsessive
initiation. *This* narrative would juxtapose
in a new explanatory way—more stable, but yet-to-be-decided—
three givens: affair,
decision to end marriage, girl drinking lye. The father
wielding his punishing panic
would be, maybe not blamed, but firmly
central, anyhow; and the au pair in this
rotated version seems to surrender to him
some of the numbing attributes plastered over her
in that letter: it's the father, this time, whose averted face,
whose unpredictable silence toward her
his near-child mistress, impress on her a violence
that is in the first place paternal.
Is this version better? Hard to tell; a
lot (the marriage, this time) isn't there, and
a compelling elegance in the composition
with the father so foregrounded and every path
through the father, though Trace loves it and feels
a basilisk emotion thinking of it, till he blushes
and feels stupid under a floorwalker's gaze,
also can't be right. What's in his hand?
He looks around: here he is in Delicacies, mooning,
and a box of French pastilles in his hand,
lettered, "Blanc MENTAL." So he folds one "blanc"
under his tongue, and then, guiltily paying
for the box, feels he's still hungry, must eat soon,
should pay attention, buy. It's wearying. Baudelaire
says that to digest natural
happiness, like the artificial kind, requires the courage
to swallow it (and then, not vomiting). This family history
that seems to omit him, feels like a nipple
through which an opaque flow of narrative supplies
that might be endless, pushes itself at him
in any surroundings, even these, and opens

onto a cool, nourishing, interpolated
landscape that might be the remembered past
but need not be that.

    Shopping, he rounds up some nice things. Besides
the pendant envelope, he buys two skeletal-heart
earrings in gold, with a thin bar at the heart's
cleft that goes through the hole pierced
in a woman's ear. At Scarves, he buys a scarf
stained with feathery mauve-and-azure
waves ("Marbled by Hand"), like endpapers.

    He keeps it up, though he's hungry, and shopping
after dark feels unnatural. Thursday evening hours. People
walk in from their cars looking pale, and almost,
for a few minutes, uninhabited, till chafed by noise
and light and the nearness of money transactions
their dry mouths decompress and facial tone
comes tugging back.

                      A third, less narrative version
of the "narrative" would happen in a room
of a hospital. The au pair girl
after four days that no doctor imagined
any body could live through, would
just moments ago have passed from "this
world" (*this* conscious world?), extinguished, and someone
comes in with the last X-rays
and clips them over the flat frosted lamp.
Someone, a doctor, or Trace's father, or her father,
for some reason turns to read them. (Everyone
in hospitals would always rather be
reading; visiting hours, you could run the generator
on people moving their lips, over magazines,
medicines, the instructions on electric beds.)
Behind him, the woman vacated by resistance and pain.
The X-ray is hard to get the hang of, irrigated
with brightness in all quadrants; wherever any structure

has slowly eaten or digested itself away
with draughts of lye, there the luminous tracer
gives its milky TV-like light, and now that's everywhere;
or at least, there's still etched only the lightest
drypoint-stroke of organic obstruction to the luster,
a childish unlettered scratch, and all the rest is syringed
with light.
          "What on *earth* are you looking for?"
in Lingerie, the nervy but bemused
salesgirl says, and Trace says, as men will, "Panties,"
meaning something more like drawers, bias silk drawers,
that would go with the fluid chemise that he
can't quite stop handling, in eau-de-nil,
"to go with this." Not since his late childhood
has he handled silk—it's sensational, like
a glinting off-green woven skin, like skin-as-web, like
—he imagines—a shed skin slipped back into, and he buys
the two pieces of it. "Do you have a break for supper?"
he asks next, and gets a startled shake of the head—
"Well, aren't you hungry?" "Yeah, I am." "I'm going
over to Howard Johnson's; if I brought back
a hamburger and fries, could you eat here?"
Another shake of the head, "But thanks." Stepping
across the threshold into the dark, he has his arms
full of flat, lady-sized boxes, four of them. On the curb,
his eyes still not making headway against
the March evening, his overheated trunk chilling,
watching ladies balance their own middle-aged
bulk across the street, flat parcels to round bosoms,
he uncasually turns back again, and with relief passes
through the glass doors into light, again; and lets the glow
of women, couples, and families lap him toward
the Lingerie woman, again.
                    "Could you show me a place
where I could mail these boxes off to people?"

She tells him how to get upstairs to the mailing desk.
"And I'll be able to send them with insurance
and so forth?" "Oh yes." Pause—some kind
of impasse reached. "Is it complicated? I mean—
you couldn't come and *show* me where, I guess?"
A smile—OK. She takes him upstairs, leaving him
with four costly boxes, four addresses, and the problem
of what's for whom? He decides fast, then writes off
cards to the women, and supervises the wrapping, and
dictates addresses, and pays money, and they're off
his hands. The panic subsides that had
started galloping in him on the curb,
not quite about spending so much money, nor quite about
obligations to so many women,
but because of deformations of the image
of himself, that might take place—had *taken* place—
in that too-broad space called "Buying for Women,"
for which read (things like), "Reparations," "Making
It—" (what? something lost, someone strayed) "—Up To
Mother," "Making It—" (her) (them?) "—OK For The Child"
or near-child, and hence, at last, "Buying
For Trace"—love-tokens, endpapers, the silk
sheaths.
        And how does he feel now?

                    He could eat a house.

4.
NOTHING IS IMPOSSIBLE TO AN UNWILLING HEART
Cissy reads that over, a couple of times,
from the narrow slip of paper that's poised
on her plate, still half-folded from being baked in
a fortune-cookie—whose undelicious halves, baked gold,
the message prised from between them, have nothing
better to do than ornament
an incidental still life: beef-liquored rice

stipples the tablecloth, the dome lid is inverted
into the pedestaled serving-bowl of unreflecting
gray metal, and the cookie plate also poses
two glassy mint candies, the bill, pistachios.
Tired and grim, Cissy's finishing two weeks
of rehearsal—and some rewriting—of "Aquarelle,"
which is a hard piece to play, and not just
because three of the instruments are Javanese.
Maybe it'll sound more elating tomorrow night.
She's cheered to learn that NOTHING IS IMPOSSIBLE
TO AN UNWILLING HEART, because hers is
an unwilling one, she thinks. She raises her hand
to, not her heart, but the small gold envelope
that's hung around her neck, these weeks (weeks during
which Trace's mother has come back to her
home, and Trace back to Manhattan to his and Dana's)
when she's been displaced in Chicago, working hard, like a being
half-awakened from a trance.
The card, when she fiddles it out of the hinged envelope,
still just reads, "I love you"; how soon that gesture
has grown almost involuntary in Cissy's pianistic
fingers, which brush over the etched lines
as if touch were a second sight. "I love you,"
like gold, is a currency in which these two
have habitually traded, and Cissy knows
some of the tides of plenitude, and debt,
and abscondence, and delay, on which the coinage
seems to float inert.
        Cissy's past 30, and an artist who knows
what to do with things, but imagine
this. A child "loves" an adult, who grows confused
by the child's advances, and loves it back,
screwing it, then panicking—repeatedly. The child can't recognize
as forms of love either the blind drive toward
the genitals, or the panicky silence; but swamped

by the adult's wild need—by its own anxiety—by
a kind of off-rhyme between the new sensations that hurt
and old, climaxless sensations it knows it likes—
helpless to turn away the new love, helpless to
accept it, helpless to keep the adult
from panicky silences or sudden inattention,
the child finally invents from its own baffled
heart a new, expensive theatrics:
a hallucinatory mimicry
of the adult, by which within the child
a second adult is made; whose function
being to put under the child's control what is strangest
in the adult and most at war with itself or the child
—things every adult has, like remorse, harshness,
stupor, intellectual longing, fury—as well as the signs
of genital desire—the child pours all its strength
into the animation of a perfect inner stranger, only swerving
it a little, always, toward an implausible childish
tenderness from which every encounter
with the real unchanged adult saps the pretense
of mimetic force. The child
whose expedient this is, changes, forgetting itself.
From a mortal trance which it wishes
always to deepen, the small anxious automaton throws
different, intermittent voices—different tongues—
even silences that aren't its own—everything that denotes
assent, but whose structure is resistance, to
the love a child can't use.
                                    A light-blue pickup truck
with Georgia plates has backed up to the sidewalk
outside the window of the cavernous restaurant
where she's sitting. It's dusk. The cab is lit
and the backs of two curly, tobacco-colored,
sunbleached heads—one bleached arm circled
around the other seatback—have the flatness,

the exotic scale, and the color of projections
glimpsed by travellers, on the screen of a drive-in.

          A story like this one
of the reluctant child is compelling to Cissy, not
about her past, but because it makes temporally opaque
and in that way visible, fragments of her present,
with Trace, for instance: her hallucinatory complaisance;
how uncharacteristically off-balance she's
felt at every node of this friendship; her implacable
anger, and the muteness about that. But more:
how much, and after what fixed study, Trace's language
has become hers, the peculiar paths of Trace's
taste. (Though, vis-à-vis,
the medium of her and Trace's relation has more
often been aphasia, as though against him her heart folded
its tongue in the night, and stole away.)

                        And more.

Cissy's a composer. Even in New York
on the subway, with music in her lap or on her mind
her outer ear grows mute; against the subway
rhythm of congestion—convulsion—then expulsion—
she studies, prolongs, and alters new
divergent strains of whatever
errancy of line will most richly, or
most barely, forestall an early interruption.
She's all attention, like a dreamer, or Scheherazade, lest surprise,
lest termination, or a dissonance she can't get that silky
inner web of herself around in time, break in; like
a dreamer, but also like a man of the world, the reader
of a novel called *Nil Admirari*, or *Never Wake*, or *Structures*.
In Cissy, the continuous plait of different voices
might be named Trace—the music of Trace—after the real Trace
whose breaks with her, whose differences from himself,
whose quick foreclosing shudder in her arms
the voices mean at once to figure within her and to

fill in, repair. And if not that, then veil.

(Besides, how clearly her recent productiveness
has a filial bond to Trace: his attraction,
through Debussy, to gamelan music; a lot of vocabulary—
for instance "walkiness," a term they've both kept using
in the midst of so much imagery in both their work of
water—"Aquarelle," "Reflets dans l'eau," lots of Fauré;
and then the tides, back and forth, between them, of ambition.)

It's dark out, and frontlets of lightning
are all over the one end of the sky
she can see. The baby-blue pickup has pulled out.
By the time she gets outside the sky's brick red.
Her hand at the collar of her winter coat
holds "I love you" as she walks. Somehow the huge middle-aged
Chinese restaurant's infected her with
a look and walk of the 40s, for an instant—the wind
tugs the hem at her calf, her shoulders are protective—
like the year her mother had her. Sketchily now, it's raining
and, sketchily, the florid store-lights prolong
their paths a little way onto the air
or spill and flare on the slicked-down street. Intermittently
it's very hushed. A car window behind her
must be open, because a top-40 song
is drifting in phrases toward her. "Walking music"
she *thinks* she hears. You're not man enough to—something.
Your ex-wife called up: a country song: children and.
What overtakes her, with Walking music spitting out
its windows, is the baby-blue pickup—the cab-light buttery
on the two tobacco-heads, who may be lost: they drive
so slow and vagrantly, with the light on.
They're both boys, she sees as they drive past,
but the arm of one still lies behind the other.
They stop with other lower, darker traffic
at a light, but when the traffic goes,
the truck sits, and their heads are bent together.

A quarter block behind, on the sidewalk,
Cissy's stopped too. Don't move yet, she thinks.
She feels like a traveller who's turned off the road.
She's back at the fugitive drive-in:
— the flat bright oblong, the lit heads,
the thriftless leakage of image, of sound.
I go for baby eyes, I go for hair that's soft and curled.
The boy's arm is making floaty gestures. A man that's like a little
boy, or maybe like a little girl.
The arm reaches back, way back, and sweeps down,
till it's reaching off the screen. It does reach out
past the back window of the cab, toward
the watcher, then withdraw — as if the boy has forgotten
he has a hand. There must *be* no back window
of the cab, Cissy realizes, or it rolls down,
but the hand, blindly, loftily expressive in
the dreamy in-and-out gesture, still looks
to Cissy endangered, as though the 3-D technique
that reproduced it must be obsolete
or trashy. Radio: I could wear my heart
to rags, making you your pretty treats; giving
you (unintelligible) walking music for your feet.

5.

Flo is driving in Brittany that day
in a little *deux-chevaux*, stopping
everywhere, but headed for St. Malo
by five. Unfortunately she's not alone;
a colleague who talks more, and much more fatuously, than
a shrink ought, is sharing the car from Paris
to this seaside conference organized
by the editors of *Thalassa: A Journal
of Genitality*. And Flo's attention is stretched
too many ways — barely pleasurable, though
she most often prefers a variously aroused

poise of consciousness. One analyst describes
two varieties of free-floating attention to
be played over the patient's stream
of language: one's like simultaneous translation,
continuous, and with regard to bits
of the discourse, egalitarian: everything means something
else; the other, lacunary
and rhabdomantic, gravitates around lapses
of meaning and wellings-up
of excess meaning, the defects of consciousness
and its aggressive floodings with remediation—
a periodic attention that seems
to say, those other moments do mean
what they say. Moving back and forth between
the two is stranger, Flo thinks, than
moving between different objects of attention:
the man beside her, say, and road ahead of her,
each evoking shifts of incredulity
that grind between chronic and acute.
She has to think about a last paragraph
for her conference paper, "Sustained Homosexual
Panic and Literary Productiveness" (which includes
close readings from *Our Mutual Friend*);
and to think (which she wants to do) about the friend
she's meeting at the conference, whose Sust. Hom. Pan.
may be—ought to be—lightened for both of them
by the nuanceless air, huge tides, the narrow
tented beach, the sense of excavation and Earth's End
about St. Malo—walking on deep walls, and the regular
thalassic irrigation, then deletion, of rocks, causeways,
fortifications, outline; to think about forgetting
to give the gas-pump woman a tip,
and more generally about tipping; to think
about lubrication; to think out her anger
at her teenage son; and all or part of the time

be semiconscious of something barely there
between her and the Citroen, sketched-in
sensations of weedy underclothing in silk.

6.
In the middle of that night, Trace—or whatever the torso
is beside Dana, damp, undecidable, with one of those
stubby, silver, wee-hours erections—seems to panic
or be stirred, trying to speak, trying to roll
over, slugging out, finally waking himself
to lie quiet with his heart thudding. What was it?
Cissy, he thinks. His mind shapes a conscious, almost
superstitious, gratitude: that it was a dream, that
he's awakened, that there's a woman with him,
that it's Dana—but he's motionless, not wanting to wake
or speak with her. Two sentences are emerging.
The rest, whatever it was, is going belly-up—he feels it—
like a dead ocean liner, full of people and surface mail—
letting drift to the surface only these
two bubbles of syntax, which, he thinks
as they clear in his mind, probably weren't in
the dream, but are some artifact of surfacing
too suddenly from the dream's pressure of narrative.
By the bed is a small notebook and pencil
which Trace retrieves carefully; but how dark it is!
But he doesn't want the light. His shape, Dana's,
the notebook's are there, but not the lines; his hand in front
of the page is repeatedly swallowed up,
and the pencil is swallowed in both hand and page
but he prints anyway, striking broadly at an oblique
angle to the felt page and the imagined lines:
Have I mentioned, too, that she was
    still naked to the waist?
But remember my position too, my own
    sense of damage and humiliation.

Even written, it's still part of the velvety dark. He imagines
two different stories that could re-embed those
distinctly *louche* quotations; but he tells himself,
to calm himself, that he's interested in the repeated
"too," an over-emphatic pointer
to ranges of continuity in the ur-dream, now lost
if they ever existed; and in the speciously, pruriently
conversational direct-address. It will appeal to Cissy . . .
when he calls her in the morning . . .

                                     Lying beside
Dana, thinking of Cissy, he gratefully forgets
that he's been frightened, and, cheek on cool notebook, patrols
    awhile
between waking and sleeping.

                In the middle of that night Cissy,
Trace's reflected self in the puddle of Chicago, is bolt awake
in the bathtub of the borrowed apartment, sweaty with unhappiness.
Partly she's lonely, because none of the people
she'd like to have with her for the performance or the night
before, *can* be with her. But she's not aggrieved—they have
real reasons—and she usually likes
nights alone: no: the brunt of this night-
long seizure is something else, more purely formal,
inseparable—as the night the day—from
the nearness of tomorrow's culmination.
(Which isn't the real culmination. For the composer,
the public première, even if she conducts it, rightly has no
more special a link to her real labor of composition
than every subsequent performance. Each should be
a specially, differently, illuminated reading;
Cissy feels that her real composing
of "Aquarelle" either climaxed at the unperceived
instant when she decided against the one change in the score
after which it later happened she made no more—

then, or it will never climax, whether in forgetfulness
or in repeated new performance. Yet she's rigid!
with affectless terror, or with something else.) Call this
stagefright. When there's performance in
the offing, with the imperious machinery
of climax after grim rehearsal, what ambition,
what neurosis, what pleasure-taking, ever detaches itself
from the hungry occasion? What work however steadfast
or love or deep resistance fails
sooner or later to lend corrosive force
to the *réjouissance* of a climax in the vicinity?
an anecdotal tide whose shallows of hesitance,
in the preparatory reflux, are close to the desultory moment
in dreams, when the burglar, having nothing better to do
than terrorize, tries to reassure
by pressing the handle of his knife into your hand
and tugging his own wrist across its blade.

7.

Over the last few years, Trace's mother has been waking
earlier and earlier. This morning she wakes at 4:30,
fills her bloodstream with coffee, cleans house until
there's enough light outside to garden by
and then, wrapped up but not very warmly,
crouches in the grass, as the long shadows take
shape, and trenchantly, impetuously digs and
prunes, often with a gardener's astuteness, sometimes too
fiercely. Since the operation she's been weak
and her side hurts: now and then, drained but galvanic
with impatience, she sits back till the least trickle of strength
returns; she's doing that when the sound of her phone
drifts out back to her just before 8. Trace,
she thinks—he's an early riser too and calls
early when he does call. Breathless and a little faint,
"Hello?"

64

Trace's strangled voice says, "Pussy—"

He doesn't mean

me.

"—are you still in bed?"

It is Trace's voice,

but whoever he's addressing is a stranger
to his mother, so, like a stranger, his mother can only say,
"Excuse me?"

"Cissy," Trace says.

"Who?"

"Is this Cissy?"

She has to stop being this stranger
who pointlessly, imitatively comes
between an unknown man and his desire.
She wants to marshal the claims she has
on the estranged address of the estranged
voice—but, in the face of an impulse blind
enough of arousal and communicativeness
to send it astray so wildly that it comes
to her, home to her, unrecognizing and
unusable, like a dead son from the war,
what hasn't already *been* marshalled?
"No," she says to the voice, "it's me."

"I'm sorry.

I must have the wrong number," the voice says, and hangs
up. But says it so numbly that she knows,
motionless over the phone, he'll have to call again
in a few seconds, needing *her* voice, needing lots
of whatever the language is that best extenuates
the flooded transfer between the two of them
of alienated excitements, of farce, of sudden power.

8.
For Cissy's half of the concert, the stage of the Goodman Theater
at the Art Institute looks a little exotic:

in their normal positions are violinist, cellist,
flautist, but in front of them, cross-legged on
bamboo mats, are players for the three
gamelan instruments. Those are three large arrays:
of bronze slabs, of bronze pots, of wooden bars:
and their part of the sound, when Cissy
comes onto the stage and starts "Aquarelle,"
is so delicate, infusing, and sustained, one note
for each beat, no beat withheld
or lengthened, a scale of five notes—so close to
seeming transparent that the ear for a while fails
in its work of discernment, fails to
pick out the fixed melody from the elaborating
lines, fails to understand how slight a token of the full gamelan
these are, fails to catch the periodic
structure since among the 38 omitted
instruments from this particular
gamelan is the range of gongs for subdividing
the periods of repetition equally, then fails
to hear any silence, any room
for the three western instruments to take shape
in, until they begin to do so—one of the more tutelary
functions here of the western
instruments being to underline by
their own differently posed invitation, the Javanese
lure into texture, a texture not of contingency
or the lapse of other structure, far from that,
but of the ubiquity on every surface
of every structure, waiting for the graze
of any tangent of attention, to grow
at once traceable, salient, thirsty. If the western
instruments in any stable way oppose them
here, it might be in that strange uncaloric
absorbency of attention, like rooty winter fields to be
irrigated by what always changes from

attention to lapses of attention.

Cissy and an ethnomusicologist have made careful
program notes about gamelan music, about the night-long
shadow plays—indigenous hero cycles or syncretized
epics—touching on the intimacy
between a deeply stratified hive of melodic
lines and the projection on a screen
of the silhouette of a flat puppet doing
something irreversible by bloody generations, tearing
the dress of a woman, killing a half-brother, or turning back
into a cloud: the narrative skimming away
from the present, and music withdrawing everything
into a deep unstable present. It would be hard
to excerpt here their account of the narrative accretions
embedding the melodic lines of which
she makes allusive use; but—what's not
irrelevant to your residual impression
from listening to "Aquarelle"—imagine
this: (Imagine this: a phrase that's turned up
before, and in the same way: a kind of chalky rag
pulled over the grammar that leads up to it,
desubordinating the new message, clouding and
fragmenting the base on which it's to
be superposed) in the shadow-theater mythology
among the distinct strata of warriors, magi,
traders, giants, gods, eagles, duennas, one
more anomalous class, of clownish servants
all aubergine-shaped, all graceless or incontinent
in their personal functions, called *punåkawan*;
a few of whom, dwarfish, unlovely, affected, happen
at the same time to be immortal.

In fact, they're gods; more precisely, they
are the wisest and, in moments of tragedy, the most
powerful of the gods. One of these is distinguished
in Javanese by being always addressed

or referred to in the plural number. Squat and pudgy
with a woman's distended breasts, an expectant
gibbous belly and wildly salient ass,
jewelry, a made up face, but in male
clothing if any, his voice tone-deaf and high
and irresolute and, as no one would have
predicted, transfixing, he wields in high
matters an omnipotence as final
as it is narrowly bounded and rarely used,
while for his life's work of stewarding
for generation after short-lived generation
the domestic retinue of one of two feuding
warrior-administrator dynasties, he secretes
a second and less couth brood of attributes, snobbishness,
a network of petty kickbacks, and an omnivorous
convulsive incompetence being the most presentable
of these. Whatever's the Javanese version of Over 22
Billion McDonald's hamburgers, that's what turns up
at the front door, in place of the desired single
she-elephant that's legendary for swerving
into battle as exposed and giddy as into
the shifting center of a ballroom.
And though *these* lapses are the lapses of
a peasant-servant, even in Olympian matters where
all this god's other constellations, those
of delicacy and sway, configure
and preside—in which laws of succession,
the transmission of codes for the classes of men, the plaiting
together of lines female and male
and divine, must by his strength and wisdom be
altered or sustained—the outcome is
not very different. The god, his waddling thoughtful step
still engorged (for the moment) with a deep
purpose just accomplished, the soft torso
heavy and magnetic with intentness, with joy,

in story after story moves away
through a forest from a clearing where
only his handiwork remains
steaming as the evening cools and
shadows tilt: it might look like
this: two sibling mouse-deer, small
hornless ruminants, each nailed
by its hind paws halfway up one tree,
the short, characteristic fur ruffled but
not broken, blood tugging against its own
viscosity to mark a trail from nostril or lips
to a stream that runs nearby from which
these two tongues have supped; and scored in
the bark of one tree, words like these: GO NOW
AND, AS I HAVE SHOWN YOU, SHOW YOUR KIN
WHAT THE FATE IS OF A WARRIOR WHO BREAKS FAITH
IN SINGLE COMBAT WITH A BLOW TO
THE THIGH: ROOTED LIKE YOU
IN SPEECHLESS WOOD, A TREE SANS LEAF SANS FORCE
ROUND WHICH THE FOE WITHDRAWS HIMSELF LIKE WIND.
    And the mouse-deer,
what overflow of totemism in the culture
leaves them high and dying here, as the symbols
maybe of some treacherous clan
the god wants chastened but not destroyed?
    The truth is less syntactic than that.
An early story about the infancy
of the *punåkawan* god tells how he was
cozened by a goddess already envious
of what were to be his wisdom and power
into taking, instead of his mother's
breast, a polished gourd with a nipple
carved in it as long and prehensile
as your pinky. From butting this
and guzzling it the creamy baby grew

round with its insidious milk, and when its milk
passed through him, there passed with it
alluvially something of his own,
leached out in the activist pulse of thirst and
supply and elimination. No one knew then
that in the thin puddle spreading from
the little loins of a little god, floated away his
memory, hot as his insides, in physical
solution: not just what he already remembered
but the reticule of any memory;
since which, il s'éloigne de son sujet
de plus en plus, the flunky immortal, and collages
like that one, particular language superposed
on an atrocity on a particular
landscape from which the god is just withdrawing
touched with state, have grown more frequent. His life
is like music—always in the present tense.
Wisdom or love sets him on his path
and nothing slows his telegraphic defile
between Chinese-high horizons, except
whatever crosses it (you might imagine a kind
of "pure" narration, all flow, every obstruction washed
away or worn through, with no author, or at least
no tendentious drift toward any hovering
obsessive image, an image magnetically loaded and reverted to
with or without relevance); no, whatever crosses
the path of the god becomes the object of
his imageless motive passion. Like
"Aquarelle," though, no flooding but is also
pastiche. At first light a warrior enemy
wakes cold and stiff from a stunned sleep
in the nest of a hillside. Inside him
his bowels are loose and hot; his numb head tells
him nonsensically, or has dreamed, that he's been raped—
and a silver trail where he can't see it, says

yes; the rolling grass
as far as he can see in one
direction oblique to the canted sun, has been
furrowed—trenched, really—throwing up walls
of rooty fabric that, now deeply shadowed, would spell
out hugely, to a high and distant viewer, WHAT
I FELT IN YOUR ARMS: CHILD THE SCOURING CHASE
OF HALF A DECADE HALF A CONTINENT
MY HEART ALMOST TOO TIRED
THE DELICACY OF YOUR REPROACHES, IN
THOSE SILENT MINUTES   BE MY ARMORY
WOMAN YOUR WINDING AND RECOILING BREATH
BITTER UNDER ME AT LAST   YOUR SILENCE
SINCE WE FIRST MET, BROKEN ONLY
BY THOSE TOKENS YOU LEFT IN MY PATH
THE FOX THAT DAY   I THINK   THE SHEEP IN THE
TREE   THE LOAMY STUMP SOMEWHERE RED AND
BUSY   A GREEN IN THE SKY I THINK PERTAINS
TO YOU AND SPEND MYSELF ON TOP OF
THEN FORGET   WHAT CHILD I THINK I
FELT IN YOUR ARMS:
                          on, like that, for acres
of rubbled dewy turf, stretching away from
the warrior—damaged, beached; also away
steps the breasted god, transfigured again.

(1977)

An Essay on the Picture Plane

I.

Canvas dissolves at a horizontal stroke.
At a stroke it is a canvas about distance:
the place is marked where things will disappear,
and what is there is salvaged from the horizon.

The vertical plane makes the absence present
to you, who are absent both from the horizon
and from the fabric itself before you
which is too articulate. Be thankful
for the absence is at least here, because it is stretched,
stretching clear to the edges, and immobile.
Be grateful too when sometimes it resolves
as a woven thing with just a woven depth.

2.

My project, really, is a street at 8 or 9
in cold weather—after all, there is a point
in late dark evening when the formalism leaves you.
Are you wrapped warmly?

I want big houses of two kinds:
in the first kind no one's visible and that's OK
where nothing belongs to it but its windows that are dark
which just reflect the night, and its windows
that are lit, which make a small transparent space, the room
that while distant is both visible and perspicuous.
For you on the street, hot and chilly:
there *are* bright places free entirely of you
and there at the same time, of course, for you.

3.

In the other kind of house is a person you've quarreled with
or come to some such impasse of desire

as would walk you past, out of your way, on this cold night;
—again, no one's visible in the lit room,

but you with your confusing purchase on the space
of fears, inflictions, and ambitions (for who
might not now walk in, putting on all the glamor
of the lit stage, perfectly irresistible,
and you out here dark, with no means
at all of yielding), I'm saying,

for you, there is no free or distant space.
Across the dark around you, the bright window is
only as transparent and no more
than this designed and speckled page.

(1973)

Everything Always Distracts

Oh Eve, help me erase those nastily scenic
afternoons with the goddamned objects
in the goddamned motel room, with both your and my

goddamned beauty; with me—your beloved—
grim, baffled, jaunty, looking
(as they say of gynecologists) in the pink,

which to us means the folded tissue of blood,
and you, dear naked girl, with the disposal of
this red explanatory lapful:

that's not our love, which is pure voice
and also a steady touch in an inky room,
making a grown man want to think

his eyesight is a costly adult disease.
Your voice, mooded and languid under my voice,
too soft, not quite continuous, not quite

your own in the penetrated dark
touching and instructing my uncertain one, which is
more simply the riddled voice of sexual desire

and, afterwards, of unsleeping tristesse
reminds me a little of the touch of writing
to the reading it inhabits, trying to sustain.

(I know you think I'm being fancy, or just flat.
Wait, though, I've got more for you.) If
it finally happens, if we discover

a night we can spend together, a night to make good
what so far is only the raging sift of the detail
of impatient arousal, it won't be more

our own than other nights. Everything always distracts,

not least on the aired and inky sheet
of our intentness. Take, say, this blind instant:

the one where your teeth clamp hard on feathers:
you're fighting tears, while down the broad half-gleaming
back the raised ass is wedged conclusively

open—and that's me. I'm fond,
identifying with your desire, of these
rooted oppositions: you being shut and open,

oral sadistic and anal masochistic,
face down and bottom up, and I
half in half out, stretching you, and taking

my own sweet, my own needy time about
going either way. I like standing in,
in unconscious magic, for your pay,

your turd, your baby; but more, I'm scared
by the scalding rush to the eyes, the rush to finish—and your
resistance to it. Scared by your pain and my

infliction of it. Scared, though, mostly by
your grasp on this now weary, infused rag
and your greed for spending me like this, but beyond

this moralized landscape of (I admit) both our desire,
your own desire extends unmet
and unprovocative. If the night finally

comes when you and I, one sleepless darkness
mimicking another darkness, penetrate
from room to room, or into breathless

room, I needn't wonder if your voice
hollows under mine, sounding delicate, or absent,
the glutted body of that voice being here.

(1975)

Sexual Hum

(April 1975)

I.

Your dreamwork, with the negligence
of schoolwork, left undone, it came
to you—the embrace—with dear explicitness

in the dream, and your not even needing
to put it in words to him, later in the dream,
"No, for I'm married," was, as things

are in James, a magnificence.
Also as in James
the blood suffusion slowly ebbed: the

engorgement, I mean, of the word
by its appropriateness, *that* fell away—of the
actual, slightly numb, and wakeful touch

of bodies in the dream, by its referent
in social daylight; all this, slowly lost,
left you in possession, when next day you saw him,

of a whole fossil history. But yours, and alone.
In the library, light gathered in the air
to fall inadequate—the eradicating light—

on, alike, non-smokers, smokers, whisperers,
sleepers, the undergraduates, the poets,
the masturbators, the two of you, when you watched

him reading, restless and like a man in James
a little febrile or tired, affecting utterly
and arresting, engaged, but not

impermeably, with his book—for it is just this play
of the permeable with the impermeable
that sets you, asimmer with privacy, to spy

on your friends, to listen lips parted as they
relate their dreams about each other, to
Sense in this theatric light Things Going On

2.

That's what should be, the sexual hum
of confusion that should, in James, resolve
to sexual desires and sexual acts
or at least to encounters in striking places
or to, at the very least, the separation
one from another of individuals.
But this one is a true confusion, not
the confusion most engorged, the confusion heavy
with love's surmise, but rather
the confusion of the absence of the erotic.
Of affective withdrawal. Of the empty referent.
Of something, perhaps, as inapt for the poem
as the failure, and for the dumbest reasons, of a poet
either to publish or teach; the being tired of rejection,
the attenuating seepage of, to say no worse,
the affordance to you of the fine careful
rapture with its hundred-proof kick
of obduracy.

3.

This consciousness, a poet wrote, that is aware
of neighbors and the sun
will be the one aware of death—of these lines, the
unagitated syntax
and ravishing obduracy make an excellent chant
for the dentist's chair.

"This consciousness," grind grind, "that is aware—"
the drill stops, the hole
in the numb tooth's shot with silver, bite adjusted,
knees unlock. "You're OK

for cavities," the dentist says, poking
another spot

"and the last thing I want is to frighten you
—it's probably nothing—but
I'd be negligent not to get a second opinion."
Huh? for a cavity?
Of course, though, for adults, there's only one thing
accorded this tone

in particular, and sure enough, "Doubtless benign,"
he adds, and in the mirror,
sure enough, a little growth on the gum.
Just as, for years,
you read and read but hardly thought, yourself, to hear
(on summer nights) avowals

that began with the rapidly thinning, hardly
credulous silence
and something, from the man, irrelevant, but waxing
every second in relevance
imbibing from your (from your—?—) recognition, relevance
till there you were—avowed—

similarly you knew at once that even this
intimacy with "probably benign"
this dilative flooding, voiding, flooding with
complicity—even this would, in time,
and probably not much time, grow banal.
Like a fresh

surprising death of someone dear
in an old war
the bitterness was at the leisure
intuited, to come:
a fact with such a future but no past.
Folded under

4.
your mild lip thus it left the office
— benign thing.
You went back in the illegible stale air

and under eyes
and staring again at the old dissertation
and two days short of twenty-five

and, with those you know, subject
to the old regime
of the play of opacity and transparence

and the relevant and the irrelevant;
to a poem that had swallowed, unperceiving,
more lives than one

and that in a week when a thirty years'
long war
could end, could not yet end.

Penn Central: New Haven Line

The future moment is the moment of guilt,
and it imposes on one, until it is reached,
the intolerable strain of remaining innocent.
—Northrop Frye

Things race back.
They wander swiftly back
around a distant, maybe invisible point
that lingers along up.

This is the Room where I catch up with my lust
hardly knowing it as mine (but *I* catch it).
But it combs so straight along the revulsions
of nature, and *that*'s a gesture I know.

Everything racing back toward status origin.
My lust and I rattling with strangers.
This motion over time is a space, that buys me
nothing. Like the love

of a man for his mother, it is not a metaphor,
but there is no making it good, but he carries it with him,
and now and again it flushes him out, in some absent sense:
other things may fill him but this suddenly always makes him
    empty.

Least of all it works in bed, which is
too relevant to be real. I am putting it gently:
what language thinks it has to do: he does continue,
and it is that bad. This motion, this innocence

that's original and not to be breached or lost
will be neither acted nor suffered: I withdraw from it
as swiftly as from these lines and apply myself with the
same steadiness to it. Never in time

because lust is tardy when it comes at all
or forward and importunate with its own sickness:
my lust and I grinding down the line divide
the second's pulse.

(1972)

Poet

Evidently there are people used to authority, who have
it in the voice, the gaze, the touch or withholding,
over everything but maybe one thing.
Possibly one daughter, or the knock of asthma.

The presence that only one desire can unstring
how little freakish it is, though, compared to you
who are absent or dispersed at times when everything that breathes
    is there
collected, who, without the mongoloid's cunning,

the journalist's decency, the spastic's self-possession,
the philosophicness even of a cherry-fingernailed girl
shouldering over a movie magazine;
who without authority where to be human is authority

have yet—in fistfuls—one authority so narrow
your voice which hardly bends the air stirs this entire.

(1974)

Sestina Lente

1.

Now helpless to, he wished he could recover the expectant fix
of the minutes before he'd been alone and able to open
his package. Compact, brown, addressed,
with his name as, he knew, he'd wanted it—in her hand—
shut hastily in the dark drawer in his desk, the box had stirred
slowly toward itself his involuntary short breath, his wake-

fulness almost. Struggling to be awake,
to reinhabit his trembled gaze, to steady all
this loss and all this fear of loss that stirred
even now (a month after the rupture had blown open)
reluctant and grateful under the girl's hand
and fantasying as firmly as he could, he had addressed

the hidden box. A ragged ear? Creepy. (Angrily undressed
her in his mind.) A nipple, red and awake?
Mutilated labia?   Her patient right hand?
Or had her virtuosity found its yellow fix:
wakened for real now, stretched, stepped lightly over anger,
spent its tigerish exertion on a poem like its turd

and casually sent the gift to him? His prick had stirred:
to be helpless, the repository of her poem!
Certainly, he'd felt more than usually open.

2.
That night his wife was out of town. He was cold and awake
at 4 a.m., knowing he was in a fix,
hunched over the kitchen table, with, appallingly, his hand

touching her gift, which was the severed head of a black cat.
Its dead fur was black and enticing, and almost stirred
this unhappy, susceptible heart which skidded and could not fix

on the small animal's being dead, or anything. He was dressed
and it was in its soft cat fur. He had never been awake
as he was now awake, while the yellow eyes were open

as he remembered seeing his silky girl wide open
in the middle of her silk, under his face or hand
or her own hand. Her cats, too, if they were awake,
he'd sometimes touched to her where she was double.
And once, impatient with how slowly they'd both undressed
he'd had, trembling, to lean over the bed and fix

on one cat's mouth his own two lips, wanting to fix and open
only the girl's lips: *then* they'd undressed by hand
and extended along one another, stirred, distended, beating.

3.
But now the machine of love's displacement is all,
in token of which he carries his cat head and his anger
and his hard-on into the bedroom. Though in this poem
I, like the man, feel shamed and off-centered by the head of this
    cat,
by the ready focus on a specious double,
we've both, I think, similarly found ourselves beating

off in its presence. Last night, fingers beating,
I lay in acid darkness of gray, etchy fix
feeling the punished organ rubbed out by its double,
my own right hand. With love, with excitement, without anger
I was looking forward to writing about the touch of dead cat
to the sentient fine-grained penis. The man silent in his poem

wishes he could recover from the world of the poem
his strangely dissolved intelligence. *He's taken a beating*
(the words come to him: climaxing on unbloody cat
he's bready, elastic.) After shame and shock and all
he falls asleep in the dotty aquatint dawn, he lies open
to the dreamed girl, his murderous girl or her double

with his face buried in her lap, bent over double
in a dreamed formal sadistic game, of course undressed,
being flogged with a stick in her mock anger.
He stands up naked, touching her arm, stopping the beating,
saying, Shit, I wasn't getting any pleasure from that at all.
And takes the stick and throws it (the same dream?) at the head of
    a Krazy Kat

who knowing the token is—as desired—from his hand
seeing stars from it, creased, extinguished, seeing double,
radiates these silent little hearts: dumb pussy, she say nuffin at all.
Dumb, yeah, but dark, etchy, appetitive, like a poem.
Or rather like the dummy of a poem, where the snuffing and
    beating
always happen, the narrative residue that's balled up and expelled
    in anger

from the real poem. Living with anger
like waking up beside a seductively mutilated cat,
can the insolvent heart do that? and keep beating
when the dream vanishes (leaving him just obscured, stirred)
from memory like the smell of the right hand from the poem.
Maybe instead it will all,

their evaded loss and all their preterited anger,
the one poem defeated, the unremembering cat,
only scrawl a ragged double crease in the memory awake.

(1978)

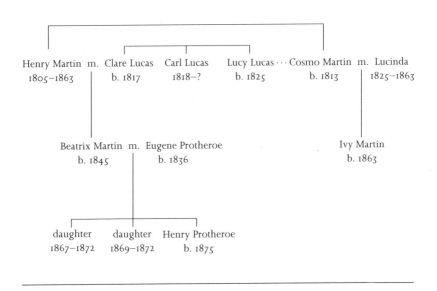

Henry Martin m. Clare Lucas   Carl Lucas   Lucy Lucas ··· Cosmo Martin m. Lucinda
1805–1863   b. 1817   1818–?   b. 1825   b. 1813   1825–1863

Beatrix Martin m. Eugene Protheroe   Ivy Martin
     b. 1845   b. 1836   b. 1863

daughter   daughter   Henry Protheroe
1867–1872   1869–1872   b. 1875

The present tense of the poem is 1880,
except where it is circa 1980.

The Warm Decembers

Chapter One.
Early History of Cosmo Martin
(b. 1815)

Cosmo Martin was a second son.
His father made as they say a killing in india-rubber
early in the century—elastic, erasers.
All the Martins were slow to mate. His older brother Henry,
then he, did well at Cambridge. He liked older fellows,
swaggered and dissipated with them, then, sodden,
numb, with the narrow lemon ribbon of
one wax candle, settled at a table
beside a window (where swarmed forms
outside gobbled their bulk from the lightless
grass, the frayed college walls) to work.
When he looked up again the sky was streaming,
watery, awful, bright, the courtyard winced
discursive in it, the candlelight was crushed, the page was
charged with a small handsome translation he did
not recognize. At twenty-one Cosmo went down.
His mother died. Henry was at Bluefields, new then,
to start to be a gentleman for father.
Cosmo did well. The brothers were saturnine,
rakes. A woman from London, Clare Lucas,
silently was installed outside the village where
brother Henry visited her in the afternoon,
not often, for eight years. She lived on
nothing in a closed house.
                              When Henry was forty
she conceived a child, and he married her.
The marriage shocked everyone: Clare Lucas was
almost absolutely valueless—

moneyless, classless, pretty no more; Henry was not
principled. Whatever the reason, he did the thing,
and Beatrix was the name given to that child.
Henry lost Bluefields to his father's wrath
and to Cosmo, and grim and poor in middle age went
into, not publishing, but Grub Street, while
Cosmo brought the profitable publishing interest down
to Bluefields—and brought a new wife there as well,
a wife wealthy, whippet-beautiful,
and coolly tubercular. Two icy chaoses,
boneless like chopped water throwing up on shore
vast canted floors of ice brown
in silky rags, mile after mile,
wife and husband grew not in one another's
affection, though, for his part, Cosmo felt
an untransmutable flat fascination
with the woman's beauty, while Lucinda felt—patient,
neglected, then, soon, jealous, ill.
Cosmo spent time away from her in London.
At the time of his father's death, though not forty yet, Cosmo was
gray and stooped, quietly growing handsome, long, a
muffled and depressed-looking gentleman
in the streets at night alone among
the hungry, the reeling inane.
To the younger women sometimes he spoke in his soft voice,
but also sometimes to a just-higher class of women,
women in boardinghouses with a little something to lose.
One night in this period
in a lodging near Great Coram Street,
the woman he was with introduced to him another lodger
whose flat pretty face camouflaged in
pebbled skin affected him, as her voice did, nude, thin,
but striated by how she had lived and where
with the guttural and the swollen-grained.
   Lucy Lucas, the woman pronounced,

and Cosmo saw at once how she looked like her sister,
Henry's wife, whom he scarcely saw and scarcely knew,
and he kept his own name to himself. The skeletal-
genteel-facetious chat was filled out by the injection
of whole jokes, that public language, by the women
(I heard about a woman
who wanted to go into St. Paul's, quite quite
nude, and a policeman stopped her—You can't
do that you know—to which she pulled herself up
haughty and said—[her voice stretching more here]—Sir,
I have a Divine Right! and the bobby said
Madam, your Left is not at all bad either, but
you *ain't* wearing a hat)—the unechoing voice
coming out the other end of little récits;
on the damson coverlet the
next night he threaded her
like a needle carved out of a wishbone.
Don't don't, she said.
And he kept her for ten years after that,
with her rent and a small allowance, secret,
lonely, and jealous. Then back at Bluefields Lucinda Martin was
at last made by consumption and by jealousy
into something that, already breathing the distinguished air
of death, made Cosmo's teeth rattle
with remorse and belated love. On her
deathbed he impregnated her, tending those two
lives, the baby in her womb, the
stranger in her lungs whose fine snout pushed
every day more through her delirious bones; until
that day when its dry feet
curled and uncurled in her dry throat,
and its heavy tail, matted with dung
and leaves, brushed in her chest,
and the vixen jaws of death gave
a yawn in her reluctant jawbones.

Death like a big Adam's apple in his wife's
throat uttered its sentence in the bare voice, in
the very tattoo, of Lucy Lucas,
     "Don't don't don't"
without undertone or overtone
     "Don't push her through":
a train in her dying vision bolted
indigestible on its tracks, mother in
one car, father in the next,
the vestibule between them parting
and buckling, the sage green horizon
lashing by in chains. Will the child
cross? No. Must the child cross? Yes. The mother
and the father, an alliance themselves of a
certain rank with a certain wealth, both insist on this,
though the child is ready to hurl herself,
the oxygenless hue of radishes, in any
fatal direction, down even, rather than terrorized
to set her foot in the coupling and swerve across it
toward the other parent. While the young railroad with
its mobility, its yawning stutter, where is it going
with the young family?
                              But here it didn't matter;
sooner or later the paws fluttered,
and now unresisting, sobbing for
the last time in her own
low, voilé voice, Lucinda hiccupped her hips.
Out at that end started an infant girl.
And out the other end its gorged tenant,
the Lucas-voiced and envious breath.

There succeeded to this a blank in Cosmo's
life, a year like those last low gaps
of Lucinda's voice, in which the sound of desire
was displaced at last, however murderously.

And when later, for the fourth time, for his brother, Cosmo stood
outside the churchyard at Lewes,
when he thought of a God, it was
to thank Him for a kind of recovery; for
work, as at Cambridge, for an escape from Lucy
now achieved, for the regard of men,
even of authors he admired, even for
a thin ice of pleasure in breathing and seeing:
   Henry's widow a matte black among
columns of bees and dust, Beatrix
at seventeen stoutly intent on her own fingers,
his own daughter Ivy leaning rigid
from her nurse's arms like a dowsing rod.

■—

Chapter Two.
Bluefields in 1880

MMMM; hmm hmm?
Trollope heard a thin voice in another room
ask this morning while he was writing,
and the same voice, a child's,
answer: *Down!* And then it repeated
MMMM; hmm hmm?   *Down!*   often, and slowly.
This, outside the French window, might be
that child swimming forward on its bench,
its lower parts overboard sideways. The whole
child escapes downward in fat
festoons, downward from its drying lips,
from the small mauve chin roughened with saliva
down and outward in soft throats, zones of
gullet, belly, almost to its
banded knees. Its very eyes escape,
spectacles swimming upward on its head
toward the winnowing hair.

                    In the beds of the garden
the palette of long autumn and dwarfish day extends
toward curdy bronze, toward mercury
that dilates on puddles, and drains the standing things
in stone. The sun drops before tea: this is
the dusk of the year, as it is of the day.
   Mrs. Protheroe—Beatrix, the child's mother—
also in the garden, and pig-faced herself
with absorption, tilting photographically
outward toward those three horizons where
all day the sun has, like Henry, jiggled, rimmed
around, glaring, and leaked from its outlines
fanning down, folds her landscape camera

at the last moment. Like the mud silt in a slow river
alimenting some passage of countryside
the view that Beatrix's eye and her camera
concoct and share, of sky, reflective and bounded,
nevertheless, though broadly passive, trains
that sky, across the fields stubbled and fouled, toward dung,
toward the flat, the blueless
aerated tones of earth—and glazed, like pastry;

    Trollope asks her at the French window, "And your
uncle?"

        "Oh, Uncle Cosmo will stay out
Nimrodding while there's light anywhere—
scouring his horizons."

                I believe it *is*, he reflects,
that hygienic when Cosmo rides out to survey
his coverts for the hunt: *he* doesn't hunt;
he's racing on now as near as may be without
pleasure; for all that nimbleness of his
on anything, at any juncture of speed and danger.
Trollope is sixty-five—old for that age—
too heavy and weak-sighted to ride, finally,
after years of hunting the most searching and almost
madly inept; his friend Cosmo, older, fitter, draws
his always youthful envy.

                  One less path to torpor.
Food, sleep, writing novels,
marriage, are the ones he still possesses,
like thin long darkness spilt
over ground, flowing at this moment from the feet of
palings, the child, a row not distant
of bulky nude trees.

*   *   *

My dearest Rose,
    The magazine, we have decided, is not to be
but here we are, all the editors, moping over
its empty cradle. And Cosmo—stiffly ashamed—
is out absolutely riding all today. His Ivy is
grown tall, and thin, brown, and pretty,
a shruggy edge in her. Had Lucinda that?
Not if I remember her. Ivy gives tea.
Gene Protheroe is *not here*, Mrs. Proth. *is*
(Cosmo's niece); why? She is fat and a photographer;
I don't like that (the latter), but she
has worked intently all day, standing, catching
trees and lawn—I like her working so.
I think they see my right arm is weak.
Now this is very dreadful to me, and
just now Mrs. Protheroe lifted from a tray
some one of those good things that women
dispense, a silk-topped finger of
puffy cake, puffier than her own, and
put it quite to my lips
gaping *her* lips invitingly, so that
I had nothing to do but eat
as I was bid. This, I am sure, without
the least pointedness! from, I am sure, a preoccupied woman.
Whatever she may be, though, she must be
scolded out of treating a gentleman forty
(say, twenty-five) years her senior as a bare,
nested fledgling, and I will.
Some others here I know you do know, young Tim
Oughton, who was to do stories, and his *gladsome* wife
Maria; old Goatey Lament, who I suppose
was playing once again with the idea
of retiring from his school for some controversial

work more weighty, at the same time more self-effacing
than what he can do while headmastering,
but, you know, he is a man very pervious to
any idea of failure; and then, to hear his name
carried with affection in the mouths of youth
is sweet to him. Indeed the new man
among us has been a scholar of Goatey's, long ago,
though Goatey studies *him* now:
have you heard of "Chinese" White? He is a traveller
and scientist and wild-animal hunter
and perhaps poet—what is he not?—and he
was to have been the *New Repository*'s particular star,
or rather lion, though he's quiet and
seems ill (all yellow, all lean;
perhaps you'd gravitate to him). You see how well
I am—my arm is functioning;
well enough for me to start *Uncle
Miles* (not the right title), too, and
I'll send some good ms. in a few days
for Flo. Everyone misses you here, my dear,
we're hardly gay at all. My love
to the Villino if you write, to
Harry . . . I think I'll not leave this till after New Year
unless you need me.
God bless you.
Your own
A. T.

"In general, everything that you think very
ugly will be good for you to draw,"
wrote Ruskin. But take this bourgeois
dining table. So much to make you wary.
In the composition, first of all:
eight adults, every one separately
a shape from the studio or the cemetery,

the men ebony columns, the women marble
pyramids, and all sparsely disposed
on the exact quad, every marker
chiselled with the words of someone not there
for someone not there. Between Trollope's prominent nose
and Beatrix's almost submerged one, next
down from his, seems miles—of damask, ham,
apple sauce, bread slabs on napkins, lamb,
cellars, the deep wallpaper: one segment
in a pattern of repeated ones.

"Do you know, now that you've woken from your nap,
how much like an infant you were sleeping?"
      Anthony is rather seraphic,
ruffling the milky whiskers that had been
tucked upon his shoulder—"Was I!"
                       "You
were, certainly. Do you mind my noticing?"
He smiles in an alert but still ungathered silence.
She suggests—"Au contraire?"
                "Yes. Just that.
You perceive, Mrs. Protheroe, that I'm proud
of sleeping with such a—a virile abandon,
proving, no doubt, how hard I have been working."
      "Have you? Today?"
                   "Maybe this minute itself,
my dear—maybe in the dream from which this dinner
wakes one, Uncle Miles was pulled across
a scrubble field on someone else's
mare, one he'd been warned about, that slanted off
rightward when it jumped—but hard and nervy in the
fields, over and over the same spot, whitening the wheat—"
      "Until?"
         "Ah!"
            "You dreamed this as I was watching you?"

"Of course I remember nothing. Unless it be
the voices of Ivy and your uncle as he came in;
like weeds in the field?"
                              —those two now
at the table's ends rustling. "But you've worked
dead hard yourself. I've seen you. Since
last night, when I met you first, my dear,
you with your light and camera have consumed
how many plates?"
                          His huge and useless laugh;
she says, "It's slow, but I'm omnivorous."
          "And Gene?" the old man says.
"I'm sorry not to see him here. I had
hoped he would join us, for the *Repository*—
though I know, you see, he thinks *nothing*
of those novels I've sent him recently."
                                        Now Gene
Protheroe has been a protégé
of Trollope's, and these words seem to Beatrix
Protheroe, bearing heavily upon
certain static confusions of
her life and heart not mentioned yet,
distinctly hard upon herself. "*I* read those,
when I do read them—Cosmo's Ivy has,
you know, been staying with us, and we did read—
with more and more admiration."
                                  "Ah. Yes?
And, here you are with Baby at Bluefields."
          "We seem, you know, the child and I,
rather to suit with Ivy—so Cosmo's kept us
here on her return. And then the neighborhood—"
Two hours later, into Cosmo's ear,
Trollope rumbles, "Can you tell me whether
all is truly easy with the Protheroes?"

Chapter Three.
Mrs. Protheroe and Some Others

The wheatfield hoofed to silver after fox,
hounds, horn, huntsmen, horses; the
photographic light that eats the plate;
Beatrix, too poor for servants, in the disused
nursery scrubbing her baby white.
Its blood flying insulted here and there under
the shock of her fingers on that boneless
rondure, and in herself
the Lucas features of her early life
now touched into one anamorphic wipe
in putty silk. From which, and from
the pursy muslin at the black dormer,
or yet the nick from tin of robin's-egg
enamel, the pinking of the coal-
light brims away. While
in baths in her memory something
is there similar: servantless, lampless
by the tub, her own mother blotted,
interleaved with color-of-blood . . .
no! No,
not her mother, Beatrix thinks. Her father.
The shrimp light breasting the tub and
one cheekbone, one browbone of the bulky
girl there, swam onto
his spotted, felt-shod foot:
all three in the one narrow space set
for the messenger (a sleepy boy
nudging, in the thickest shadow, outward
against the door his plumy, toppling
head) from the *Weekly Review*, come to fetch

The Letter from Italy, which Henry Martin
dictated beside the tub to Clare.
Cavalieri e amazzoni a un Cross-Country,
moist snow—surprise—all'ippodromo di
Tor di Quinto, *le gratin* enjoy
il Restaurant della caccia alla volpe;
we thought, the other day, of Shelley
when with our guide and colonello Slade
we watched il bagno dei bambini
di un asilo.

             Father should be asleep.
Clare and five-year-old Beatrix usually
did their work and their own toilet by
the blearing, then the blinded, coals
in the hours after his "sleeping-draught"
torpedoed him; but not seldom there were
nights, like that night, when after tumblers
and tumblers full, lungs pulling stony through
the length of thrown-back torso in the dark,
in the dark finally his eyelids rose
over the trepanning outraged
regard, dull brush of nacre, still awake,
awake even while through the soft palate
unnerved by sleep bleated and bleated
his lower body's breath. Unbelieving, finally
"*I*'ll wash the child," he'd voice.
A few fresh coals woke the resentful fire;
the red-gilt tub, for once, was warmed,
the child among her father's fingers more
and more wooden, deeply chilled (as when
he gave her lessons, taught her, later, how
to calculate, to translate, how to speak):
if at some such moment a messenger
should come, from the *Review* or *Quiz*
or daily *Quidnunc*, for the night's copy

(which might be Characters of Widows, Strange
Laws of Orientals, Beauties of the Lake
Poets, Is Painting Dead?, On Girls
Today and Dangers to Their Health, whatever would
spread thin and make bank of
those earlier travels, glum years at Cambridge,
and now a strange facility,
the child of delirium and cant),
the little family that had come into
legal existence, economically
exploitable, plastic, declassed, only
perhaps in order to legitimate
this fretted potentially female nudity
in the tin tub, was saved, again, saved
for the next day with its own trickle of light;
cold meat; raw mist; hot drink; sleep denied;
with its rainy glaze of the paternal
words, its own vision glued to the
lanky blotted slippers of felt.
What, in all that time, did Beatrix
understand about her family's
status and history? Nothing was kept
secret from her or revealed to her;
the things she put together were both more
than wanted, and less than at any rate
Henry had feared. It was from Henry's fears
that Beatrix learned things most. To learn,
meaning at once *to be passive* and *to
be feared*, to have a power never, at
the same time, under her control or in
proportion to any detail of herself,
became a transcendent appetite (transcendent,
i.e., insatiable, because of that detour
around the quick unlandmarked spot
marked simply, on the map, éclaircissement),

unproportioned as the link
of her cold dinner to cold tummy, or as
the snap of her father's hysterical hand ˎ
at her ears, to the expensive languid
vocalizations this enforced. Half-ignorant,
makeshift, absorptive, thus, Beatrix
grew up, clumsy to the eye, genteel
to the ear, mysterious to herself, because
to be a woman, what is it if not
to serve the purposes (labor, display,
mobility, verbal recuperation) of a
particular class? Beatrix, almost
lost through the very coarseness of
the family's social weave, to class, almost
also escaped some of the waste of sexual
resolution, almost, except for the
imprint of violence.
                              In novels
like *Great Expectations*, where the hero has
to come to terms with origins in the working class,
there are prerequisites. It must not happen,
first, until the child's speech is already
distinct from the lumpen-vernacular. But by then,
by that, the child's adult: he has enough
delicacy not to like (not to
be able) to concentrate much on the
conditions of populous need, the condition
of wealth or comfort. Solution:
a serious illness, delirium, debility,
from which he is nursed as one newborn—
as one born with speech, and trailing clouds
of heavenly correctness, long before
the disarticulated muscles stream
together again expedient. It was
in some such way that Beatrix finally

came to love, to perceive, her mother (or
her mothers, by that time. Things changed
outside the little space, just as
a puddle of night in a hollow
of bright lawn, all day anxiously deforming,
eccentric toward the grassy lip at dawn,
then shrinking southward and into the roots,
and then, at noon, like mercury, dissembled
to winking atoms, bridling in the afternoon
one little knob, brimming from that
up every grass to where the golden shield
of the evening crushed it level—this plot
of striving shadow, daily rolled around
the grassy mouth, never could it reach over
those shallow hummock lips; not, not by the breadth
of one fine blade; never, until
there leapt across the spread of grass and air
writ large, the earth's shadow, darkness, that had
no shadow, but washing downward embraced
the pool that leapt up into it. So
throughout the chill, ill-assorted family
tided the changes of the greater family);
George, the old patriarch, had died;
Cosmo Martin, with new cheap editions
and two of the wildly popular monthlies, *Acid
and Quill* and *The Ingle Nook*, was printing money,
or all but, and the war in the Crimea
was fine for india-rubber, in which
some of the Martin money had quietly
remained. For the first time, the elder brother's family
had something from the wealth—the kindness—the now obliquely
tendered concern of Cosmo: they lived
in four rooms, not in one, and they ate better;
though whether it was as the family of
Henry, his brother's brother, or as the

family of Clare, her sister Lucy Lucas's
sister, that the small remittance
flowed to them from Cosmo, I don't
know—what kind of gesture it was
in Cosmo, growing richer, stiffer by
the year between his cloistered women,
and childless, still, at that time. Be that as
may be, the money came in some respects
too late—too late, if saving Henry from the stamp
on him of desperation was a motive,
as it may not have been: the long, phlegmatic temper
in both brothers, the something *eng*, tightened
in Henry by the squalid quartering
with Clare and Beatrix, sometimes to blows,
the grafting onto his organism of the bottle,
the seamless glassy inaudible hating flow
of the idée reçue, by which this distrustful man
supported his early brave choice of life
were irreversible: only the things
extraneous to those melted away
as, over years, he aged.
                        Two weeks after his funeral
Cosmo sent to Beatrix to wait on him
at the Bledsoe & Martin offices. "Perhaps,"
she offered as she entered, "it was my mother you
actually wanted? *I* am Beatrix Martin."
Cosmo was shocked: to think the girl lolloping
at her father's graveside, painted across the face
with pollen and tears, or alternately, quite
absent, ignoring her mother, had really thought herself
invisible to him?
                "Oh, no. It is you.
I could not intrude on her right now. Besides
—I hope you won't think me the fussiest of old
widowers—I felt somehow, exchanging

those few terrible words with both of you
at the funeral, that you and I
might even more usefully talk between
ourselves, just now, about the fate of your
bereaved household."

"Oh. As to money, I know nothing.
Is that what you mean?"

"That, but also other things.
I do, you know, know something about the money,
so we shall be able to talk of that." The girl,
who seemed to herself to be incapable of learning
the one genteel art, how never to
be rude unintentionally, lowered her chin into
her round neck, and looked out at him.
"I know," he said, "my brother was not a wealthy man
because of acts of our father's. Surely he had
nothing to leave to you?"

"Nothing," Beatrix said.
"Surely not," he continued. "And yet you know
that you are to count on me for a continued
income. I want to tell you that. But, having that,
what, still, are you to do?"

Beatrix was too confused
between thanks that died at her lips, and a true
perplexity about her mother and herself.

"Your mother:
has she spoken of anything?"

"Only perhaps
to mention her sister, my aunt Lucy Lucas.
Aunt Lucy seems to have a little money,
and they have spoken of our making together
a new home. But I, I scarcely know my aunt."
"Oh. Is that true? Do you truly not know
your aunt? And yet—I think I've heard—that she is
very like your mother? Are they not close?"

No one, Beatrix thought, despairing to explain, no one
is close to us, or to women like Aunt Lucy,
whom you, Uncle Cosmo, if you ever met
any such woman by some chance, would feel
for days that you had had hunger and secrecy drinking
through your bones like straws. "Close in a way.
I suppose the plan might work."

                              "Because—here, I shall
tell you a thought I've had, and yet more than
a thought. I have made a purchase."
("Slowly now," the girl thought, still suspicious,
but already almost in jubilee that still
there might be a life for them.) "Kincaid, an agent
of mine, has been at this work for days, travelling,
you know, 'to and fro in the earth'—really
everywhere. A house, I thought, a large one,
with rooms for boarders—that your mother
and her sister perhaps might live so,
as owners and keepers of the place;
a healthy spot, I hoped, too, an airy, dry,
salted place near the sea, wholesome for women."
"And," the girl asked, "has your agent
found such a place, wholesome for women?"
"He *has* found it, Beatrix. A house in Gt. Yarmouth.
Today I bought it. Now I wish to give it to you,
or rather through you to your mother and her sister.
Their income from it might be £400
or over, and their own rent found.
Then, I see it likely to appreciate,
so the thing seems respectable to me;
and to you? May I give it you for them?
Will you talk to Kincaid about it?"
                              And
to me?   And me?
         In Beatrix's nerves

there was a hubbub so unleashed in bitterness
she felt her uncle must feel it (no,
he didn't; in fact, a kind of stucco
of raised beauty fingerpainted her, ungainly,
florid, at such a moment, so he felt
startled in his self-esteem, that she was there,
and something more than a conduit to the sisters.)
The clamor was terrible. Hearing, sight, equilibrium,
smell, her ramified spine, every sense
atremble with its own head-voice singing
in its own deaf music
no to being a slavey in a rooming-house
to making common cause
with those impoverished lives of females;
"Uncle," came at last her voice not her
voice but a reedy fasces, "What
of me?"
       "You?"
          "What do you mean
me to do?"
       "You?" He gazed more blankly even than
he felt. "Why, nothing."
        "Nothing?"
          "'Do'!
Do nothing. Beatrix, are you so much
as seventeen?"
      "I am seventeen."
"But, seventeen! Nothing but a great child"
a great rococo child
         and so to Yarmouth
the women travelled, little enough going
with them from their London lives
of comfort or acquaintance. One night
before the white low house was even half
filled with boarders, Beatrix, wearing only

her sturdy dress in gray, her oatmeal shawl,
nothing but a pound or two about her,
moved out along the London road and did
not turn back.
             It was August.
          Father, she thought.
The dome of St. Paul's spread silvery
over her inward eye to welcome her;
under her feet the soft earth breathed shortly,
as she did. Short and violent bits of languages
she'd learned of him for his plagiarisms, spoke
in her, "Geboren in der Flucht," I almost
stifled in the smoke, "Des Vaters höchste
Furcht die an das Licht gedrungen,"
and while she could smell the ocean she tore
to the west, the moon behind her
inking the sandy road ahead of her
and voyaging even faster and more
silently there. It suited her, to be
nothing in the negligent
and devious light, meeting no one, not
human, silent—her father
would have said, she imagined, like a horse.
One on San Marco—gilded, scored.
Dull traces of the harness.
Her haunches brushed with mercury.

Chapter Four.
The Girls with Buttons

At the darkness of every night of her
destructive elopement, the girl,
never respectable, reviewed
the losses in respectability of
the day: the little bread she'd begged,
the greenish hands in the mantled pool
lifting curtains of water up, the walnut
membrane of exposure tugging at her face
and all the indignities unanswered:
these things, what did they weigh?
beside the moving, blindly as she knew
it was, against that pain. Then, also
in the night's great room, over the finally cool clay,
the never thirsty enough clay,
planting her puffing feet apart on it,
squatting as if to listen to it, down over it,
the current of will so little tolerant
of control, will so local
in the distended bladder of this
woman too shy (of course) to urinate in the light
and air, was let to lapse;
if you think that *is* a lapse
when the fire hose in the Alabama town
slips away from its focus on the slick Black woman or man
who is suddenly averted, who's dropped as glistening offal
on the street—the water's eye
washing itself away; nevertheless, the current
in a beheaded coil, wavering and swollen,
rounds on the troopers in those wrenching pulses that
could pull your legs from under you like

the running noose; Bea's control, let out
of her control, it played, the burning, banked-up piss
on the uneven ground—splitting—changing its note.

    Swans, cows; in the sloppy landscape anything
condensed in front of her.
                         Not only the land
and the water, or the sea water and the fresh water,
but the water and the air, over and over the same places,
sometimes invisible and sometimes visible.
Falling asleep under a windmill
she thought she'd glimmered onto in the dark
(the short, incomplete night)—
she woke, curled up on her side, in the light.
The creaking noise she still heard
was a cygnet—climbing up and down
on top of her. She could have hugged it; but
lay still. There was no mill there. The mother
with her long, vapid neck, and her white back
mounded like the chalky downs of the south
had snatched from the rolled-up hem of her
oatmeal shawl, in her fist relaxed open,
the little lump of bread for the morning.
The mother swan, who had no teeth,
who had no lips, even,
or cheeks,
tilted her great hard craw upward
to the continent violet sky,
playing the hard crust back
in little clacking movements, till it was
gone. And more came; swans everywhere, like clouds,
like inexpressive, overprecise clouds
that could not change in shape.

    Of course, the escape was not made good.

    Of course, Beatrix grew ill.

    The one big urination after dark,

after the long summer day of control
that became both easier and more
accompanied—loosely accompanied—
by pain, soft ignorant twining nosy pains,
began, every night, with more reluctance.
One night she could not do the thing at all.
Another night she crouched waist-deep
in the near-opaque channel of the Broads
in the dark, and stroked her own hair, comfortingly,
and murmured, till, out of a pure bladder of self-pity
the rush of liquid strangled through. Through what
she did not know. No woman knows where
her urethra is, but only some
hot floating place, at other times
imperceptible, somewhere between uterus and clitoris.
(Translation: Utica and Clinton, N.Y.,
and between them, New Hartford [*mine* sinks], where
in the parking lot of one of the super-discount stores
a Chevy Malibu sits. The time is Sunday morning,
minutes before opening time, at noon, so that
the steering wheels have people parked behind them
in the scattered cars, some of whom certainly
are noticing the extensive and steamily beautiful
wetland view from there [in fact
these blighted parking acres always have
the loveliest—giving a center, ugly, nonsensical
as it is, and a direction, to countryside
whose beauty floats like oil on its meanness,
weighing it down, vexing it, aimlessly].
Balanced on the patient exhaling knees
in the car, a notebook is open,
its loose-leaves spread. The leaves conceal
a patchwork of stickers, postcards, clippings [an
inquisitive plaster dog, in armor; Trollope;
a freckled sow with piglets; and so forth]

that lines the inside covers. One, a real snapshot, shows
two little girls, one fair, one dark
[as Jarrell begins his beautiful poem]
in identical outfits of — 1952,
say. The dark girl, who might be six, wears hers
invigoratedly. The fair girl, half her age,
is being chafed under the armpits by
the waistband of her jumper, by wads of sweater sleeve.
The dark child is heads-up. Her slender jaunty legs
are crossed, knees cocked, to make a lap in plaid
for the display of a big-headed round kitten.
[Indeed, handwriting on the back that's slightly like mine
names this composition: "The girls with Buttons."]
The three-year-old — no neck, the crossed legs only stubs —
sans pussy, what has she in her plaid lap?
Her hands. Which hold each other and her gaze
as if they were anything *but* hers.
The fictitious absorption of that gaze!
The little squinch of brow, shielding her eyes
from sunlight coarse as straw that animals
have been curled up on and disarranged, the rounding
of shoulders saying no to a coltish red wagon
near the gravel driveway, the patience with harsh grass
where her skirt is not pulled smoothly up
under her — how slavish it all is,
yet, at the same time, it is independent.

    For sisters [we are sisters], the chisel of emulation
may be hammered too smartly in — we did that — but
the ancient configuration, women with one Buttons between them
needn't *always* spell the silent and the fatal.)
    For there the sisters were
when, a fortnight later, Beatrix woke
at home (in Yarmouth), undelirious.
Lucy was wiping clean the long
outbreathing cleft between her great sick thighs;

Lucy, the little sister, almost openly a whore,
unified and hard. Clare, Mother, was before her,
the older girl, stained dark with fatigue,
the girl whom responsibility made brittle.

The sick child's eye, more one now than her body,
her ear, lapped in the unsolicitous cockney,
plumed and un-plummy, of the two water-birds
about her; her own tongue which she could not move;
her pillow which commanded a view of her domain
but not the obedience of a single atom of it —
these she almost resigned. These, the Lucas care
and the healthy-for-women seaside air
preserved to her. The sisters, at such an early
moment in the hotelier career
for which they'd neither preparation nor
any aptitude save a willingness to survive,
a friendliness (little indulged) to money,
Clare's homing instinct for the grim, and Lucy's flat
ingenious vulgarity, worked for ten;
so up the VACANCY sign was slapped again;
and after awhile, up to the attic sickroom
potatoes were being carried in their skins,
then down without. Also, up on the whited walls
Lucy or Clare would fix with pins
texturey little landscapes scratched in chalk
by the invalid's fingers. The English field
her imaginary subject: fields
with sausages of flab; or foliage like eyebrows;
or grass the fur of an animal
too sick to tend itself — possibly one
even whose old distracted claws
hoed at its own numb sides;
like the Beatrix Beatrix perceived,
extents of vital texture, slabs of it

only at the last extremity nipped in
to make an animal form.

It was this sloven woman who, becoming yes
a slavey in the rooming house, also
made her way back to London, more than once,
to Cosmo—who let her represent
(she being genteel-sounding, diffident, and in
the dark about himself) the women, to him.
Imagine her there on the sidewalk
leaking expressiveness, like Dr. Johnson;
fancy Eugene Protheroe, the young critic,
meeting her there, the imposing niece of Cosmo Martin
of Bledsoe & Martin, his new publishers.
Their London wedding. Cosmo responsible.
Baby Ivy running in tight circles.
Clare, and not Lucy, there, well-dressed, and mute.
The husband (no one quite knew this) mad and bad
and volatile, fascinated with his wife,
degrading her compulsively, depressed,
enthusiastic about expensive things
for short, terrorizing periods
(photography was one of these; she moved
into the rubble of it), coming at last
to gambling. Money, once scarce, ample, then
scarce and for good. Two daughters died.

                              A son,
Henry, born in the tenth year of marriage,
now (1880) looks like an immortal, though:
at five, torpid, nihilistic, giggly:
and, possibly, depressed.

                    The Bluefields nursery
this midnight, as a candle tiptoes in
unfolds, like gauze consumed by moon
or moths, or simpler darkness,

toward the one small swathed-up bed
visible only in patches (the Sussex moon pulls back
from the window as the candle comes,
the huffy shadows pull around them all
their inexplicability and bulk,
and the yellow flame itself
is no friend to a hasty eye);
yet, catastrophically, it does grow visible:
under the curtains, tapeworm swags
of indigestible linens, all thrown up
at bedfoot, and great Baby on top of them—
halfway up the bed—entirely beached—disposed
like the stove-in carcass of some ship
or mill, bleached white as sails:
head-down and hulking discomfort.

                           "Hen,"

his mother breathes. But no eye opens.

                              "Hen."

Downward the huge head burrows to more sleep
among the ribs of bedclothes. "Don't you," she
offers inaudibly, to no one, "want
to be under your covers?" The little lips breathe, "Oh."
"Oh," the lips breathe, tucking themselves downward.
The etchy lids don't stir. "Mother," he forms.
"Oh, little Mother, I get so—
discouraged."

                   Then suddenly the ugly-duckling smile
flashes itself most graphically at her.

Chapter Five.
Wives of Great Men All Remind Us

Fast and loose as it is cast, the net
of masculine filiations tugging part of its length
through Bluefields this warm Christmas, is
no light affair, although, like air
from the diffusion of daylight, inextricable
from the showier presence of women. As though
Martin were the strands—Lucas the weave?
Other versions of this, bright Lucas wool
on Martin canvas, Lucas figure on Martin ground,
visual warp and woof, or obverse and reverse, either make
the women sound too purely ornamental
and optional, or else the relation, XX
to XY, seem symmetrical, as it is not;
for consider some examples of it
among the people at the breakfast table.
Their links, for instance, with Cosmo, their host,
most originally on the ground of his huge fortune
and inclination for capitalizing with it projects
of literary ambition, are now made visible
in florid female life—Bea, for instance, representing
the firm's investment in (the absent) Protheroe,
and herself gaining in value by it.
One person to whom her representative value
seems intensest: gray-haired Tim Oughton, the novelist,
at thirty-three (her junior) fresh-faced and eager of throat
as a plump hound in training, when Eugene Protheroe
pronounces his books good, and Bledsoe & Martin publish them—
long small romances, of a delicacy
whose grain his charismatic prose may swell.
His wife, Maria, who's lovely, does not breakfast

(as if she feared too early talk might blunt
the affectingness of her remote
swimmy diffusion—the woman is,
in her one body, far from stupid, but whole
gradients of violet distance), so
Oughton feels he has his whole attention,
the attention of the coffeepot, the letter tray,
and all the possible plans for the day, to spend
on chatting up the other. Trollope too
feels something similar. His links to Cosmo,
who does not publish him, strike with a more
knowing root than money if not a deeper,
and a practiced one, in each of them,
as one might say of Boswell and Johnson;
also, he is a man writing a novel
and so needs female types. The one, the tight bouquet,
vernal and resistant, of the English
girl, Ivy is, to him obviously.
Her very gaucheness with the coffee shows it.
It makes, he thinks, greatly for the potential
of a high compliment, through her, that will
be really pleasing to Cosmo, in *Uncle Miles*
(or whatever that book is to be called)
—he does it well, her fragrant type, he knows.
Her eternal foil, the Mrs. Somebody,
though, is the one he much more now enjoys:
the Mrs. Somebody who in the important
item of actual husbands has always
either one too few or one too many,
and who to the hero (for whom she is the latter)
appears in some climactic scene with gun
in hand, or whip—before her fine renunciation
joins the poor candid lad to the spriggy girl
and banishes herself.

                    Always in the background

of this ambiguous woman, a man who thinks he has
the ownership of her is physically abusive,
or has been. And, in the novels, that history
slices, in its effect, in two directions:
first, that no such woman every may
be an object of actual blame;
second, that no fresh fortune ever smile on her—
that frank, manly English youth, specifically
(the creature so common in Thackeray and Trollope
that one begins to name him: Frank Manly, English Youth)
must at whatever cost in adventitious deaths
of minor characters, nerve-singeing woman-
to-woman visits, and the unstanchable emission
of drafts, revisions, and alternative
versions of letters, never make her Mrs. Manly,
never let the violence that she
now necessarily embodies, mark
his stripling life, or leave an image on his family
legally visible.
             If Trollope sees
Mrs. Protheroe as this second woman,
suppressing certain other perceptions of her
(for Mrs. Somebody must be beautiful,
inhabit all her body, and be suited
to ocular domination—and our woman
is of course not so), that's possible
because he is *not* Frank Manly, looking at her,
but an older man of avuncular regard
(tied to her through her uncle, indeed, his friend);
and the other link too, maybe more important,
helps him make this extreme, romantic casting:
for, much as he admires Gene Protheroe
and the impetuous, self-ignorant thrust
of authoritative judgment in the younger man,
his protégé, still, he has easily imagined

the potential in that for violence—against
one's own, and one's own women, most readily.
Now, as he meets the wife, and as he finds he likes her,
the image comes so strongly that it must be so.

"Trollope, I've a note here from Lord Twytten."
"Yes, I thought we'd hear from him today—
some cottage child who saw you yesterday
on horseback, would tell Humby, who'd tumble
to tell *him*, that as a working party we're a failure."
"Does he hunt today?" Tim Oughton asks
(he and Maria have brought salmon jackets).
"No—not precisely. But he writes that Humby
wants a little bye, down beyond Southover,
and any three or four of us are welcome
('so long, adds Humby, as they holds their tongue
and comes up prompt, and this time the young gray-haired man
keep his horse *off* of the houndses tails'—)
don't you," Cosmo adds, "suspect
Twytten's invitations to us are mainly pretexts
for made-up Humby insults? However, will you go?"
"I'll go," says Oughton, "and Maria, if
she's fit—unless—?" and darts at Beatrix
his extra-heavy-lidded glance. ("Not I,"
she murmurs.) The schoolmaster, Goatey Lament,
a wonderfully roly-poly man,
sitting at the breakfast table drinking coffee
like a blowfish with a hole in it,
adds, "Not *my* go, certainly."
                              "And White?"
Cosmo asks him.
                              "Oh, for Chinese I won't answer.
No doubt he could doze all day. Or else
he'll tear off like a madman, and throw his jangled frame
into some excruciating stony place

and botanize, or write, or smoke hashish, and sweat."
(If you don't know Lament—if you didn't go to Harrow
either with him like Cosmo, or under him like White—
try to appreciate the spasm of extravagance
and admiration behind such a remark
from a man as timid, as compulsive as
this fat sweet moist-eyed master.)
"You, Trollope, he wants for something more delicate,"
Cosmo goes on, "he says. Some affair of a dog.
'Humby asks for a nursemaid for a hound, he says,
what's addled like. Not sick, but addled like.
Would that red man (note how he doesn't say
gentleman) what don't ride, but what hunts,
care for a short considering walk with Miles
(Miles may be the hound) to cast an eye
at him? Sensitively he adds, if not
so be, there's Toby Page to companionize
the poor mad dog, as Toby be's himself
also, one gathers, addled like, although
with a more sadder idiocy.'"
                              Oh dear.
Cosmo—Mrs. Protheroe—do you think
I really have to babysit this dog?
Oh, dear Mrs. Protheroe, you haven't said
where *you* mean to be today. And yet
in very truth "I do like nursing beasts;
perhaps I've even said as much to Humby
within the last ten years. Do they expect me
at Twytten, with receiving blanket, then?"
"No. He says they'll drop it over here,
and then go on to Southover."
                              Also—to pace
one country, with another, novelistic
countryside unwheeling
its own rutted lanes and pompous rides

in just that same, conscious place; to be
in mental flight from the sustaining presence
of someone one is with, back toward the scene
of fiction, and its creatures one loves?
Surely that's joy? The scene—
I imagine lying beside one man,
and thinking about the other man;
or on the train to Utica, which is like home
because of working near there, to New York
which is like home because of a husband living there,
I look out at the Hudson (say it's March)
and then down at the notebook—
maybe lines about ice for Ch. I?
At the family party in Queens, my mother pretended
to her mother, that I'd never remember
the streams of home-sewn identical-sister dresses
from our childhood. "Oh Nanny, *I* remember."
"Those tattersall jumpers we took pictures of,"
my mother said, "at the park?"

                              "No no no,
on California Ave.," I said. (A friend who met
my mother said I wasn't like her,
but did say "no no no" like her—"No no
no, *that*'s not what I say," I insisted.)
"At the park, and then later in our street,"
my mother said. "And those turtlenecks—those were
the very first turtlenecks." (The first we had?
The first in Dayton, Ohio? The very first
in the world? Before the French Existentialists?
But here I am with my grievance—)
"You know, in those pictures, how Nina has
Buttons in her lap? And me—"

                              "You *can't* remember,"
my mother interrupts me, "Butterscotch."
"Butterscotch?" I know that's Buttons, in the snapshot,

the one I'm writing about.
          "Sweetheart, she won't remember,"
Mother and Daddy look at each other fondly.
"You see, we got two cats when we got Buttons.
Some little girl came door-to-door with kittens,
so I thought—one for Nina, one for Evie; and yours
was Butterscotch."
      "Why?"
          "You had the same coloring."
"But what? Was I too young?"
        "No no. But Daddy said
he thought, two cats were two too many.
So finally we compromised on one—
on Buttons. Right, Lovekitten?"
         "*I* thought
the two were two too many," Daddy amplifies.
But driving back across the Triboro
with Hal, the sky is silted up
with low, retarding marks of lava.
Just as we came to the bungalow in Queens
my mother popped out of the front door.
Her little sister popped out the side door—
they were both in sundresses Sissy had made;
they were almost identical. It was so cute.
We didn't know which door we should go in.
My father tried to take a picture of
mother with Sissy's daughter—their little shoulder straps
kept ticking down off of their little shoulders.
Two lefts—one right—slender and fleshy—two rights—
Out! out! for air—
never to be the captive of one consciousness—

In Trollope's novel: Lady Dwindle nodded
off, dead to the world, while Ellen at
her morning-room desk had the photographs

disposed across it, masked in glare, inexpert,
novel. Uncle Miles cross-country taken from
behind, his mount a blazing white-or-black.
Miles slouched (sketching?) in a victoria,
the slack horse's nose to the ground, the ground
a dragging white, like the sky, with moist snow,
weeds breaking through the space like puddles,
a heapy fence, no horizon, an edge of hill.
Here, at the beginning of the novel,
Uncle Miles is already dead, and
the wheels in the photograph, stapled with
a white rust, and the inkblot hill, the view impaired
here blankly, there stammeringly
with fragranceless, invisible stitching rain,
—Miles himself among these things is looking
like an object of attrition. "At Charades":
a third photograph shows him gap-toothed
and looking massive, in an outdoor group
in costume. Cricket, lawn tennis, the Faerie Queene,
bambino, pirate, blandly handsome Indian—
all squinting. Miles is wearing a gown. His
décolletage in white gauze gives onto
undiaphanous, bulky throat and breast,
teeth splayed in a big jaw, and that
fair complexion that bright sunlight
seems to congest and mottle. A tossed salad of
sky is mounting behind them, and at their
feet—in assorted shoes—in tufty lawn—
a woman's hand has inked, "14 November."
Meaning to Ellen this party At Charades
will be, a few days later, after hounds,
and Miles fallen among the skidding hooves—
which his long, weighty limbs survived unbroken, only
the weak heart stopping.
Under the photographs, a note in the same hand:

after hesitation that I send these to you,
but I do send them to you, as they are
of your uncle. They were taken in Florence.
Rachel Hatched.
            The ugly name in fluid writing
was not quite new to poor Ellen:
of a Mrs. Hatched she had indeed
heard—heard much. The hesitancy, even,
she felt she understood, so much had she
guessed of the woman's standing. Moral, from her youth
and the narrowness of her experience
which had been so far merely to lose
through early deaths each single deep attachment
of her heart; conventional, contractée,
similarly—as the dimensions of herself
had shrunk from family to the merely singular;
yet she was of an angelic courage, and would
(Lady Dwindle feared this) not for many years
remain conventional. The crepe, the rigid depression,
these would wear out at last. Would not the girlish super-fineness?
And yet she had sent Mrs. Hatched no letter,
nothing so far for her extraordinary gift,
as if the girl had taught herself to feel
that no such woman might be touched without
the certainty of defilement. Not the less
for all this, was the gift extraordinary to her.
After the losses in her closer family,
this uncle, the half-brother of a mother she'd barely known,
had treated her with kindliness. His image,
slipping like an iron forge overboard
into her heart, had rearranged in silence
the level of its flow, changing its visible
hollows and its opacities. The fast, romantic life
of moneyed fatuity—his wintering in Venice,

his meeting the same people again and again
in different countries, and seeing statues and churches—
these, the things he told her about
in Regent's Crescent, lent him a crushing magnetism.
Something else she'd inferred from a friend of Lady Dwindle:
how Everybody knew when inviting Miles
that Mrs. Hatched also was to be invited
for overlapping weeks—
how was *she to feel? The thing mattered,*
almost cruelly, almost fantastically
to her, and no less later, when Uncle Miles
as well had joined the troupe of shades.
So that in the shadows of the photographs
the one woman strained at the contours of the other
—to trace, to recognize her, not to miss the pencilled news
of her fulfillment.

*   "At Charades," a tiny serif,*
a shamefaced round of cheek and chin, was tucked
under a male disguise: black owlish spectacles,
the hooky nose of a Jew in wax, a smudge
underneath it that looked like authority
—unless it were a curd of female pinkness—
bodied in pigeon-breasted gabardine
of pseudo ragged cut. Earlocks. The photograph,
painterly almost in the English style,
as if the resistant early winter light
of the Veneto had steamed in, orotund, with its spots
of visual rhetoric mysteriously condensed,
like an astigmatism in global geography,
and had come in its buoyant procession
around to the front of the camera, and moored
—old precisions of summer blinked from view
for good—the photograph, pretty and ostentatious
as light declaiming flesh could make it, shed,
as glazed fur sheds the weather, Ellen's fanatical,

her humble investigation:
even the intimate London light in the morning
room abstained: was this a woman?
Was this woman, that woman?
companion to the bulky, handsome man
got up as the Blessed Damozel . . . ?

"Oh! Mr. Trollope!"
"Mrs. Protheroe. I expected to find
each of our party somewhere, if I wandered."
"But I thought I was hiding very shrewdly—
anyway, from the hunters. I'd determined
on taking a whole day alone to shoot
the Priory ruins, and this morning I thought,
what a good place for foxes not to come to,
so I came now. But you would know: was I
quite wrong?"
                    "Oh—altogether."
                                        "*Would* a fox
want to come here?"
                        "Who wouldn't? Even this
poor alienated pup has nosed you out.
I'm sorry, though, if I've disturbed you."
                                        "No, only
give me a minute. I was really startled.
How is the dog? Is he so very sick?
He looks beautifully glossy to me,
with all his lemony tinge—unless that's just
this odd solstitial light?"
                            "No, hounds can be
lemonier than this, even."
                            "Is he demented?"
"Demented! Well, I hardly know. I *don't* know,
truthfully; I haven't been attending.
My heart's been off in novel-land. The hound—

he's followed me. Or, really, I should think
I've followed him. At least, we've accommodated."
"Perhaps you should go off again?"
                              "Oh, no,
I'll simply tuck your apparition into
some corner of this dream, my novel."
          "Oh! how peculiar it is."
Beatrix, who could look like Mr. Pickwick,
mixing the fey and stately with the direct
and deadly, never *merely* flirted.
                          "What's peculiar?"
he asked her. She was thinking.
                        "I think *I*
had a dream, with *Trollope* in it."
                        "*Trollope?*
What do you mean?"
                    "I'm just now remembering.
I told myself as I woke, to remember."
"'Trollope,' spelt how?"
                        "I didn't spell it.
                                    I think
it was a kind of pudding, like blancmange."
"My dear." Trollope felt actually shaken.
Which kind of Trollop(e) was it? Then, it seemed
a liberty, to make one into pudding.
"You ought to tell me about it."
                        "Just hush a minute.
I *am* remembering."
                    She stood quite silent.
One of her hands found the other.
Her gray, Athenan camera gaze fell
toward her fingers, held before the bank
of bosom, the bound high waist.
"I don't know when it was, but it was in
Yarmouth." And, below

that line of firm intentness, stood
her creased and fussy lap in oyster frieze—
"I was talking to my mother and her sister
about an earlier time, before my father's
death, when we'd been to the races. We had stopped
at the railway station buffet, that time,
for—for bloaters. But now, my aunt Lucy
said to me that there'd been a mistake
or misunderstanding then—that my father hadn't
meant to pay for a meal for *me*:
'We know Harry was very wise, but—'
she began. I broke in, furious,
'*I* don't know my father was very wise.
I hardly know *anything* about my father.'
I felt awful, like an infant. Then
my mother began to speak.

       I can't reproduce it.

       She said two things. First, that my father had
always disliked me. Even that he still did.
She said this with satisfaction—not maliciously
toward me, but feeling
that any, any vestige of inclination
in this dead man, especially of a
feeling so opposite to the grain of nature
meant that he was not spiritually
quite dead. He was still real. She said
that she had felt at first that this,
his being dead, was just an intermission,
that he was waiting for her behind the scenes,
'in six months' time, or another six months.'
But now she didn't feel that. Only dislike
for me, could anchor him a little longer—

       But the second thing she said was different.
It was that my father's taking against me
had been meant to conceal something the opposite,

a strong underlying desire for me, stronger
than for her, than for anyone—and that
she was bitter.
                        But, again, that she was grateful.
That the whiplash of hatred and love for me
might, she thought, keep him a little
longer from dispersing in that death-
that-comes-just-after death, when the spirit
so far nearly intact, though fainter and
subtly off, or subtly tendentious—struggles and gives way,
losing its resemblance to the lost person
and even the desire to resemble him,
and is no longer even the spirit of one person
but, suggestible and promiscuous, drifts apart,
worn to the very atoms of the stuff of soul—
    Then my father came in, canting.

    That's where the pudding came in, too:
he carried it, one-handed, and it was called a 'trollope.'"
    A white, oh, an architectural mayonnaise,
rounded, and swaggy with arabesques, and huge
but not by a long way so broad as its glaze plate
which it was so forgetful of, the sucking rift
of pudding pulling pudding. Or—
again, frighteningly he would remember
that he was holding it,
the hard rhetorical hand underneath
struggling to find the center of gravity
slewing across the tipsy platter when
already it was broken meat, burst dimpled milk,
the protein girdle ruptured,
or almost. "And the phrases:
well, it was what I said before:
the pudding, it was like his knowing he was dead
and so becoming 'absent'—while he raged on and on,

but then like his *forgetting* he was dead, so that
the spreading turbid place of the thing he didn't know
touched on the spreading turbid place of that
ruinous thing my father thought that it
was he who knew; the phrases—"

come,

      kiss me after breakfast, with the coffee
screwing out through the taste of bland
rosewater, and the dead breath of milk
puffing after it, and after that
your own most intimate sour,

  come, cunny, singing with me
on the *bateau des supplices* with all the choirs
drawn raptly through the streets—to church—
in bliss—

      come with me

           go with me

                 move on

but think how *odd* I feel, dead here, and standing
like a bride-boy in my anal tuxedo—

Chapter Six.
Blissy

"A little learning is a sometimes thing."
Beatrix that evening sits almost stupidly
at the piano. Like horseback, this
is a late accomplishment, since marriage,
something learned in private out of duty
to Gene's ordinary, delusional ambitions.
Ivy is singing, "Batti, batti," and the two
have practiced this together; still—
she might as well never have seen it before;
she might be following like hounds, by smell.
Cosmo, not a little lubricated
after his dinner, murmurs on
at his friend Trollope: "Look at my daughter, jerking
that melody out of her throat like a,
like a, tapeworm."
                           Trollope is watching Bea.
"I wonder how she got it into her,"
Cosmo is going on
inaudibly. "Poor antsy dear. As they say in France."
Beatrix's puffy brows are vexed
together, with the same hapless
play that, Trollope's sure, the brows
of baby Henry on the pot display,
the one that infants use
to signal effort, wind, or flannel
desire, or that in the marriage bed
(he pictures this) the mother shows—
mind off in another place entirely,
blood swarming with all its business toward
her middle, and the whole centrifugal/
centripetal fray only visible

in trouble of the fabric of the brow.
(While baby's dimples quiz like new,
like freedom, every time—the mother's brow reveals
after all there will be only the two
little plays: condensed together, displaced up,
and the place of each of these
papered in a permanent readiness
to flinch, to underline.)
   It's Christmas Eve. But desultory
except the little beam of love and dismay
from Goatey Lament to his recumbent protégé.
The school's a desert now for Christmas: Goatey
remembers with a bump-bumping heart, though,
soon everybody will be back in place.
The same way that in hilly countryside
it's pleasing and notable how promptly
that west hill rises to the mark,
surging to meet you *soon* at (the obligatory)
eye-level, though sooner or later any
horizon will meet you there, this spanking
frontal one or any common long-
withdrawing pencilled lowland—so
for a headmaster the narcissistic
equation is terribly exact.
Does it sweep through the whole circuit of the long
form rooms of all keen, ruddy children? —or
another year suddenly it's answered
early and in a single shape
a little gallant oh-là-*là*
when the rod is taken from the cupboard.
   Of the individual loves, Chinese
was not the first and not the last
but most circumstantial and profoundest,
in that small earth whose poles
were at one end a ritual of punishment,

a culture, at the other, of doleful (Horace) and
beatific (Surtees, one another) quotation,
and the certainty of wealth and neglect
everywhere. The small day-boy proletariat
(Trollope had been one), mostly muddy and unenvied,
how it had spawned this elegant square-jawed
young gangler, this inspired, easy student,
semper brilliant but also almost semper absent,
was unimaginable; but when the typhoid came
to their cottage, the headmaster entered for the first time,
out of love, and found
the father dead already and the mother
dying, and five of eight children lunging away,
and two of the sick, the mother and Chinese,
also suffering what even Lament finally
recognized as delirium tremens. Yet the boy
survived it all—the gaping motherless
day turning over and over into
soft motherless evening with a steady voice
moving on through Robinson Crusoe and the Faerie Queene
and not, even when the boy rolled over
("I'm not asleep") to sleep, to irretraceable
logics spinning out inward toward mother,
ever stopping. Blissy. When the master sickened
back at Harrow the convalescent read to him.
My goody, imagine that great barge in sheets.
A heavy swell? Oh but immensikoff.
The huskied high voice mended off and on
at the text, Cowper's "Task," or Coningsby, where
Sedgwick the Etonian head-boy's
manful, selfless alacrity made
this fouled, Harrovian sickroom eastern-seeming,
somehow, bewarmed and bricky . . . still,
as Goatey's chins would stubble onto Goatey's breast,
the adolescent voice would cease on the instant.

Now, at this instant, Chinese thinks, I'm happy.
In this hideous English room at least
I'm not dying, the way I was in Agra
at Dr. Garg's beautiful English hospital.
A fortnight in this room and I would smother.
Ten minutes of G. gazing at me like that.
If Tim Oughton gives tongue again.
But just-this-minute lying on the couch,
a Laggy Dog joke unreeling from
Miss Martin, once upon a time there was
a man who had a retriever he adored;
he travelled everywhere with it. On ships
the dog would get a stateroom of its own.
The man had his place at the Captain's table,
the dog had *its* place at the Captain's table.
Once they went to Australia, though, and the dog
got lost. The man was disconsolate!
He forfeited their passage back, and stayed
a *year*—looked everywhere. No dog.
Finally he came home a broken man.
Five years later, he's at the Observatory
in Greenwich, strolling, trying to restore
his shattered spirits, still, when he looks down
over the Royal College and across the Thames.
And on the Isle of Dogs
he sees a bounding, golden speck. It's coming.
Toward him. And getting bigger. It's a dog.
It's just the color that's imprinted on his heart.
It leaps into the water and feathers across
and shaking itself on the nearer bank
and barking, it runs toward him.
                    And? her father asks.
                              And, Daddy,
it was *almost exactly the same dog*!

and at the same time turning the pages
of a photo album from the table,
aware of Mrs. Protheroe's piano eyes
trying to penetrate invisibly to every page;
they are her pictures of her family
(who bribed Baby to bring this out? Tim Oughton
did, probably), of Gene, of Baby Henry, of—
Chinese has headed back toward the beginning:
someone else (Gene) had been taking Mrs. Protheroe
herself, badly, grimly, holding on behind
the neck of an exquisite girl child:
the cheek of velvet underneath the cheek of rumpled
silk, three puffy hands that can't let go,
four light-colored hating eyes cemented
on the camera, the tiny face speaking for the huge face
a closure as of eyes that fit like little nuts
into their unfinished sockets, and the mother's face
speaking for the daughter's face an amplitude
of light-catching small impressions, dints of pity
as it learns slowly to withhold itself, of fear of violence,
dints of patience, patience, floated on blubbering tears,
bright dimples of visceral connectedness with the child
who's dying—also the hammered glare of the new shy
art winking with pink Gadarene
defiance to the uttermost.

    Of course, as orphan Chinese reads
the photo, it's the mother who slips as mothers do
away, the child with awful heroism
locking her like a glacier in its arms,
tugging her back toward it and making gravel of her.
    Chinese, the teacher's pet.
Home from the East and sick and under teacher's gaze
hesitant to reach for his tablet of OpalEne
Restorative, a taste he owes to Dr. Garg's
solicitous attentions, his thoughts scrabbling toward women,

asymmetry snowing down like a wolf on the fold.
Me, when I lie beside a man,
K. C., and think about another man,
my husband, Hal—
or, really, often I think of James Merrill and David Jackson,
the only happy marriage in Western literature
practically. And why? The phantasmic woman,
the necessary misogyny, these are so little central,
so delicately misplaced on the gorgeous stage of men
who, as women can, love in ostentation and reticence,
in full memorious narrative polish—these
are the very gods' pets:
the gods saying, that's right, that's beautiful,
that's exactly what we *wanted* you to write,
you and your four friends, whom also we are
insane about, and who are also *us*,
and if any of whom happen in this life
unfortunately to be females, well, when it gets down
to Essences, in the afterlife, don't worry:
everyone gets to be a man in the afterlife.
Just take care of each other, as much
as you can, stay lovable, *keep pen to paper*.
    "*You* lovable person," K. C. sometimes pronounces me,
or, as if this were news, "You're O.K.!"
Or, "I *love* you. And I also love
Harriet," his wife; "I *do*. Is that possible?"
Oh, dear. If the things we do for love were banal
as the love we do them to compel . . . !
Further in the Protheroe album, Chinese finds
either the pages growing more peculiar
or his own edginess . . . over the rim
Maria Oughton, her hand in a gesture of pushing back
from her face the heavy hair, arrested, only
the violet eyes in tiny meaningless saccades,
sweat pressing from the upper lip—of course

he knew the instant he met her;
there are styles of addiction that greet each other;
long sweet childish dialogues of permission
fearfully heard by the child of some other interdiction.

    I Ching says about *The Warm Decembers*, "Peace.
The mean decline, the great and good approach.
Good fortune and success."

Chapter Seven.
Epistolary

Harting, Petersfield

Dearest love,

    And I'm to be without you for the New Year, am I?
Flo and I bear up wonderfully under the blow,
as well at any rate as buttered tea
and little greasy mutton tête-à-têtes
and other comforts as you may imagine them
afford. Truly, anything you do that *isn't*
editing the *Repository*, is splendid—anything,
I say, is splendid, *but* do not imagine
I can't already tell
that Beatrix Protheroe is to be the "new
Kate"! (we have a letter here from the real Kate)—
but, that you *will* always have some girl to love you
I do know. All's well, etc.;
Any, dear, pray make them coddle your asthma and arm,
and pray, *pray* don't strain over *Uncle Miles*.
More cigars have come! Ever lovingly your own wife
Rose

P.S. I know you've meant me, this long time
to write to Mrs.—Mrs. Cross—love and congratulations,
but, Any, dear, *would you*? I feel the awkwardness! Miss Evans,
Mrs. (fancy "Mrs.") Lewes, "George Eliot," now Cross,
and he our Harry's age almost—
Please, dear?

Bluefields

My dear Mrs. Cross,

    Rose, as you know, is the scribe of the Trollopes
for the ordinary occasions of our friends,

as, births, deaths, emigrations, novels published,
bankruptcies, and the like—but this year I am snatching
from under her (figurative: I'm from home for Christmas)
but none the less for that inquisitive and well-wishing
nose the most splendid of our end-of-the-year pleasures,
the greeting to you marking, my dear, such a year of changes
as positively gives even your gloomy friend
(for as your friend it's been, you know,
gloomily or not, or enviously even,
my honor to see myself, long years with you in the sisterhood
of novel writing)—hope for any amount
of reinvigoration, of adventure.
You have, and Mr. Cross has, our most loving wishes
for your art and well-being.

    Here, there's been a funny story.
Lord Twytten, Cosmo Martin's neighbor here, has had
living with him for decades a factotal creature
named Humby, brought up savage, doglike, and unfurnished
as is, of course, Twytten himself unfurnished,
doglike, and savage; well, the story got about
somehow of Humby's having read and brooded
in secret over—can you guess?—*Mill on the Floss*.
And someone asking him about it elicited
information that indeed the book had quite
finished the fellow off "as to his finer feelings"—
yet, puzzled him, as well. "That part where Maggie and Tom's
dead, of a sudden, in the flood? And then—
equally of a sudden! New people!" Humby grunts.
"New people! someone speaking! some weazening sooth-seer
named—is it—Latimer? And his wife I can't remember
from anywhere, hardly, in all that first part of the book,
that greenish woman: no doubt she was there,
but can I drop my finger on her? No! And it was strange. . . ."

and on went the critique. You see, of course, the problem!
Some nasty, no doubt American promiscuous edition
somehow washed up at Twytten, that the creature would
have scavenged from my Lord (what *don't* they share—
their bottle-bottom spectacles, their medicines,
the hounds, their mounts, their "culture")—had in it *unmarked*
"The Lifted Veil," printed after *The Mill*—
and just so had he read them! And to whatever mind
it was that read those narratives, it hardly seemed more strange
moving from the one cluster of names
only barely, in his doggy way, at best
discriminated by their—what—their certain smell
of the characteristic, to another—*barely* stranger,
just palpably stranger, than in the first instance
possibly to be *reading any novel?*
"Almost"! The man almost remembered
Bertha rising in seaweed from the Floss!
Such unpredictable rebirths in new editions
must we not now, dear Mrs. Cross, anticipate.

With my dear love,

A. T.

In the novel:

Regent's Crescent

Dear Mrs. Hatched:

Regent's Crescent

Miss Ellen Chapman sends her thanks
to Mrs. Rachel Hatched, for the photographs, but regrets

Regent's Crescent

Oh Dear Mrs. Hatched
    My Uncle
    You and my Uncle
    We're coming to Italy! Wait

———————————

London

Dear niece,
   Trusting that you may be at home,
or that Mr. Protheroe will know to send this.
Beatrix, I have a question for you.
The person writing this for me, the girl
Melanie, my maid, is also concerned
in the matter, which is delicate—
it's so much easier for me to dictate,
though, than to write, myself—
still, hoping you'll be candid when you answer.
It's this, niece. I have grown attached
to Melanie, rather, who is a child
from nowhere, or she won't say where—
like your mother and me and our poor
brother Carl Lucas running off from Staffordshire,
and Carl already half-deaf and half-insane
from the potteries, or how could he
have dared, even your mother not so much as twelve—
and like us, after Carl disappeared,
the girl has made what shifts were *to* be made,
and clever and grown up not so pretty, run away
with some money from an abattoir,
which money, for awhile, she lent to girls,
but still it wasn't much:

I found her treating with a shopgirl in a shop
and liking her voice and clothes I asked her
to come with me. And we suited:
she was glad for a steady place
with a female who didn't mind that she'd
money to make on her own time
and, it might be, a life on her own time,
and who would have her taught to write and read;
and I needed a maid and a girl to like.
I like this one. I feel that she's like me.
And if she's not soft, she's patient,
pulling off and on my feet (which hurt me
almost all the time) my shoes, and willing
to talk with me about the shoes I like
and the shoes she likes, et cetera.
The reason I don't mind her plainness
is that she is French-looking and closed
like a door, very spare, with a little nose,
and careful about her dressing,
we get on, as I say. But,
and I don't think I mind her hearing this,
not wanting her to run away from *me*
with *my* little mattressful of cash,
and wanting simply to make it worth her while
always to *be* patient, and to stay
by me as I grow older and,
I imagine, not nicer to be with,
and as she says she has no name
and would like it, I've been thinking
of adopting her to be my daughter.
What do you think of this?
I don't mean only what you think of this,
but I wish to know about the money:
niece, if you are thinking daughters come expensive,

you are right, and as you know I've meant
this nest-egg, little thing, for you—
I don't know how you stand. Is Protheroe
solvent? Does he support you? Shall you leave him?
Will he support you then? And Henry? Shall you stay?
Or if you left. . . .
I don't suppose it's merely my imagination
that makes me ask these questions, Beatrix, although
for all the word I've had
from *you* on this peculiar subject!
Well he is your husband isn't he. But think.
If you find that you will need the money,
not that it's much, you'd better tell me now,
for otherwise I want it. Melanie,
I know *she* wants it. And I guess you know
by now (pardon my French) you catch more flies
with s***, than sugar.

                Hoping to hear from you.
  Love, Niece, from
           Lucy

                    Bluefields

My dearest Kate,
   Rose will have written to tell you where I am,
improving what dead pretext—well, it serves
to pry me for a week or two away
from doting at her side,—which makes her grateful—
and then, to circle as if festively among
the little mistletoed levée
the "Ivy'd" wreath (Ivy the permeative
ornamental, colty daughter of
Mine fully equine Host—old Cosmo, whom you know),
a cincture of all sorts of bonds

whose substance, and whose satisfactions, I don't know
that I was ever young enough to understand,
gives something *like* a pleasure.
But one that you, my dear, need never feel to be such,
you with I hope your warmer egotistic pleasures,
for who . . .
Yet even from this "Balzacian" point of view
how little I do know your pleasures, Kate!
Or much beyond the journalism you send on,
my warmth of love and hurtful journeyman critiques
propelled across the ocean at you (I've
more than one feather, Katie, to *my* boa).
Perhaps, there too, it's winter?
I feel that I don't care
how soon the sun sets here;
I'd thought to die in London, but the hour
grows late, the old fowls gape into the farmyard,
while yet the fabric of the light is durable—it seems.
    (Kate I wanted to mention—it's of no
importance—Rose has teased me about a woman
here, as "the new Kate." I grind my teeth!
I fancy her writing of it to you!
As if any nice young woman whom a man,
foolish and old, incline his ear toward, be
a "Kate." Ignore it! It's of no importance!
Has not one always anyway with Rose
about all the women I'm fond of, a consciousness
that, somewhere, A Tone is Being Taken. . . .)
God bless you, my dear.
                      Your own—
(and if she write you of it, you *will* know
not to be agitated? "Beatrix"
is nothing—though you'd *like* her, *that* I'm sure;
her lot, which another time I'll tell you of, is one

that seems to make especially on the female bosom
a call the most mute and penetrating for compassion—)
Your own, my dear, with special love,

A. T.

Bluefields

Humby—

    So it is Lord Twytten's groom, you are.
I knew in Oxford St. the night you said
you were a Lord-knows-what for Lord-knows-Lord-
who, from *Devonshire*, that you were lying,
and shall we meet again? Cannot you get *excused*?
Do you like the graveyard of St. John's
I think it is I rode through yesterday,
the stone with the dog agape on it, or did you mean
avoiding me? If so, pray why? Eleven sharp.
I am more than ready. Here is my whip.

Chinese White

Chapter Eight.
Two Arts

To have been depressed in early life.
Imagine the child wetting its bed
(and say the family's poor, the beds are shared,
the washing's done in buckets and by hand,
the drying sheet smothers the attic room)
whose crazy father then decides:
This is a child who "must not" be given water.
Or, that it's dangerous to let this child sleep.
The awful logic nods only when he does —
and then the parching child nods off
in sleep that's only waking, waking.
Waking to violence or the expensive wet
that makes violence. And say the child survives
and finds, somewhere, an art.

Waking in the morning, I remember first
I'm grown up. I have some money and a car
and anything I want, to cook and eat,
and (in the horrid, doggerel blank verse
in which I — no, not "think" — but breathe, and represent
continually to my own ear the place
of my unthinkingness) repeats, repeats
some vapid version of a Shakespeare phrase,
"Yet Edmund was beloved."
Waking alone, yet E— is beloved.
Also: "an important writer of
fiction and poetry, — "
$\qquad\qquad$ of *criticism*
and poetry, of course it's meant to say,
but "fiction," in this empty register,

scans, so "fiction" in my head it always *is*. (You see,
just by the way, how it is that hexameter
means mana, freedom, grace for me with this compulsion.)
Waking as an adult, now, who has an art.

An adult, I mean, who's not depressed.
For whom a vacant, distended, paper-light globe
called "gratitude," fills up the inner space
(gratitude as it were for water and for sleep:
for being able not to loathe "the sweet approach
of even or morn, or sight of vernal bloom,"
"or flocks, or herds")
—gratitude without an object, too, since these
good things—love of our life—
are our own true birthright if we've *any* right.
Gratitude, *positive happiness*, not the less for that.
Positive, meaning not good necessarily
either, but—now surplus, outside. What
isn't, although it must have been once, me
but now is rented or is lent to me,
is paid as wages for the "work" I therefore "love." I do,
I "love" the work that lets me like the world,
"love" the indenture that I call my "gift,"
almost as much as simply fear
the blinding loss of it.
                              "Loving" in truth, I take its shape.
(But what that is I won't be first to know.)
Sir Richard Burton, on his first exposure to
boy prostitutes—to, in fact, the "execrabilis
familia pathicorum"—wondered why
whole boys commanded almost twice the rental
of young castrati. —"The reason proved to be
that the scrotum of the unmutilated boy
could be used as a kind of bridle for directing
the movements of the animal."

                        To have,
as excess, the thing you might as easily not have
propels you forward with the impulse from behind,
the place you cannot see but others can.

Tonight—it's past 11—in the graveyard of St. John's,
Chinese the mysterious and Humby the mysterious
play at a game like this one.
The tough old whipper-in, catamite and familiar
to tough, ancient Lord Twytten
lends to the drugged, imperious boy his seamed
voice, his leathery obstetric hand,
at . . .
          Oh, at what?
                    At "sex."
                              At a game of *horses*?
Can that be true?
                  Another Henry I know
says that the thrill, for him, in watching
video porn in the bar's back room's
the irrepressed consciousness that somebody
somewhere (Upstate?) is busy wracking brains
to figure what on earth it is that men
can Do Together.
                   It *is* strange:
the way the art of our necessity
   makes precious, the vile things—
the finger's-breadth by finger's-breadth
   dearly bought knowledge
of the body's lived humiliations,
   dependencies, vicarities
that's stitched into the book
   of The Sexualities, wasteful
and value-making specificity.

          "I feel convinced,"
wrote Trollope, "in my mind that I have been
flogged oftener than any human being
alive. It was just possible
to obtain five scourgings in one day
at Winchester, and I have often boasted
that I obtained them all."
    "Looking back over half a century,"
he added (with the doggedness
of the adult he made himself from the child
whipped far beyond the reach
of "perverse" transformation at any psychic
exorbitance, of pleasure to
himself, to his tormentors even, from
what Dr. Middleton calls the Grecian
portico of a boy),
"I am not sure whether the boast is true. . . ."

Left by his mother in the mother's place
his murderous father's bloated punching bag
("knocked me down with the great folio Bible")
—even yet, loathly afterbirth, to learn somehow
in his excessive thirties
a possible desire, possible and infectious,
for stories in which bouncy rationalists
are let however briefly or tragically to receive,
to embody with a sibylline humility
and briskness, the afflatus of the Bureau
itself—postal inspector facing down
the postmark forgery! entails unwound!
solicitors who know solicitors
who know the law on heirlooms! —and clerks,
clerks by the score, into whose equivocal sails
may breathe or may not breathe the zephyrs of ambition,
competence, real engagement;

against a background where another
figure is let horrifyingly fail
in the common work of giving face
and shape and color to some want.

It isn't always possible. I fear it for myself;
I see it in the body of Beatrix in the bath.

    Neither abused, myself, nor a member
of that best established Clean Plate Club, the poor
in my family's last generation—still
this is a narrative that I
—if it *is* a narrative—
that paralyzes with self-reference.

Neither abused nor poor,
"Imagine me" (in a Brontesque locution)
imagine, an entire year
in the life of a person and her talent,
not depressed, a year and more—
gone; just gone, the almost spoorless
consumption of this basilisk narrative
if it is a narrative, gone since
the penning (pencilling, mechanical)
with an arousal full of promise to myself
and my production, "'Loving' in truth, I take its shape."
And what that is—the grecian portal of a boy
or man, the rococo of Beatrix in the bath
whorled like the painter's day's-end palette, the finger
however loving that sets the harmonic glass
to vibrate—and that stays it—
the finger however loving on the string,
the string's however swollen bite of the finger.

(The year, I tell myself, not wasted, lets
me take to yet another academic venue

the touring company of my favorite show,
Landscape with a Frieze of Assistant Professors
—the one where the near-burnout women faculty
realize for the first time that we'll never
be loved, *always* be feared, by these departments,
and, that that can be called "fun," and "power,"
when we decide together that it's powerful and fun,
able to leap short colleagues at a single bound,
to be thought in conspiracy whenever
two or more of us lunch. ("Oh, really, nothing.
Girltalk. You know. Lawsuits, Title IX. . . .")
Almost myself a bouncy rationalist
I'm pretty good at this, "love" it, and send
postcards in our code to my little brother,
"Not Depressed.")

But still
the writer herself has been transfixed.
Whether by that premature intuition of success
early in the chapter, or by the lordly yoking to it
there at the surface where I draw my breath
of the submerged and wreathy Medusan sister muse
melancholia by whose silence and rebellion
gagging on coral—comes, at best,
I guess any buoyant illusion of
the ordinary joie de vivre.

Two arts that feed as one.

Fat art, thin art.

Not iron, but the tin thrust in the soul. . . .

Note on "The Warm Decembers"

The Warm Decembers was less than half its intended length when, between 1984 and 1986, I stopped being able to write it. It's clear that chapter 8 of the poem records a crisis in the writing; still all these years later I can't specify what the crisis was. Except for one big shift, at any rate, my sense of the poem's plot remained pretty stable during the decade (roughly 1978–87) when I thought of it as current work.

I hope you wonder what was supposed to happen?

The 1880 plot at Bluefields was going to hinge on Trollope's seeing Beatrix, one morning at breakfast, offering a bite of food to Tim Oughton in the same intimate style in which she had, in chapter 2, offered the lady finger to himself. On this equivocal evidence he concludes—rightly, it happens—that Beatrix and Tim are involved in an affair. The perception agitates him in ways he incompletely understands. His habitual solidarity with Gene, his little *tendresse* for Beatrix, impel him to stage a scene of clarification that he vaguely and wishfully imagines, in advance, will bond himself and Beatrix more closely together, at the same time somehow persuading her to go back to her husband.

What he doesn't get, besides how mixed his own motives are, is how completely at bay Beatrix already is. She knows well what Trollope has allowed himself to gather only in "exciting" intimations: that the violent and crazy Gene Protheroe is not someone into whose charge she can return either herself or the child. It's mostly hopelessness, inattention that have involved her with the banally narcissistic Tim Oughton. The dominant feature of her present state is sheer paralysis—and I was looking forward to writing about a connection between that paralysis and her almost unnatural productivity at a landscape art that ("passive," incorporative) successfully displaces or delays her sense of initiative.

The scene with Trollope, then, doesn't turn out as his barely entertained fantasies would have had it. Beatrix is frankly panicked.

"Will you return to Gene?" Trollope finally asks her. Her only response, "You've made it impossible for me to stay," reminds him uncomfortably of his self-flattering advance scenario, in which the same words might have been uttered—in which she was to have been no more than flustered by the inexplicit pressure of a supposed mutual desire, and they'd have parted with sentimental renunciations. This is unhappily, obscurely different.

Strange how clear some parts of the poem (like this particular denouement) were in my mind, how murky others. What Beatrix is going to do in her panic is . . . to elope with Chinese White. "What did I once think these two would feel?" (James Merrill wonders at an analogous juncture.) Beatrix's panic, Chinese's druggy opacity are supposed to explain everything, but I can't remember (if I ever knew) how. They will have connected, anyway, after the evening described in "Blissy," when Chinese suggests to her in private that he knows how she may be able to sell some of her photographs professionally, and she leaps at the thought of a move toward financial autonomy. I can almost see what's in it for the desperate Beatrix; but for Chinese, especially at the moment he's resuming his promising games with Humby? In the plot as originally conceived, the elopement was to mark the end of Beatrix. Someone will "hear of" her a few years later, in Tangiers—and after that, nothing. Implied: squalor, desertion, wastage.

The one big change in my plan for the plot came here. I was at work on *The Warm Decembers* in the mid-1980s—at a time when phobic narratives of "the shadowy bisexual" were being, for the first time, hideously explicitated as part of the new common sense about HIV transmission between gay men and the supposed general public in the United States. Involved in such other writing projects as *Between Men* and *Epistemology of the Closet*, I was finally developing the kind of jarring alertness that many other people had had for a long time, to the dynamics of spoken and unspoken, the detailed and the blurry, that are liable to circulate in the neighborhood of any such spectacularly scapegoatable figure as Chinese White. While I imagined that drawing characters like Goatey, Humby, and Chinese might open up some new spaces of gay representation — especially in the context of nineteenth-century realist narrative — I also came to need a new sense of the *structure* of the thing, something far beyond the implied, presumptuously conventional "what more need be said?" about Beatrix's future with Chinese.

The future I imagined for these characters remained sketchy, because by this time the actual writing of the poem had come to (the excruciating state I will euphemistically call) a standstill. I found myself unexpectedly seeing Humby as a character with another life and a future, as well: doffing the comic rusticity that had hardly ever been much more than other people's weird fantasy about him, in a few years he was to abandon Lord Twytten at last (there was going to be a little flashback about their boyhood together, too) and live with Beatrix, Chinese, and maybe the child Henry in London. The Humby who is to make the crux of this new antifamily is a new Humby, an extravagant figure now known as Dowager Jones: away from Twytten he no longer seems to resemble his master, but grows grave and queenly, with (my notes specify) an exquisite *porte de bras*. Reading Neil Bartlett's brilliant book *Who Was That Man?: A Present for Mr. Oscar Wilde* (London: Serpent's Tail, 1988) several years later, I recognized my fantasy of this ménage in Bartlett's descriptions of Alfred Taylor, Charles Parker, and the boys whom he describes as constituting "something like a gay family — a group of young men who worked (as blackmailers and prostitutes) from the same premises, slept together, sometimes for sex, sometimes perhaps because there was nowhere else, and sometimes lived together, casually support[ing] one another. Mostly they were low paid or unemployed (servants, out of work valets). But they dressed in splendid drag, held parties, and when the money was there, they got themselves taken to the seaside, taken to the Savoy for chicken and champagne, they received silver cigarette cases and silver-topped canes, gold rings, and pawned them when they needed to. They offered Oscar a different city" (p. 157). Of course Bartlett's book was also a reminder, had I needed one, of how starkly the attempt at such an evocation would have exposed my inadequacies as a historian!

One possibility I had in mind was that, over time, there would have come to be two, interpenetrating antifamilies in London: a female one comprising Lucy Lucas, Melanie (now Lucas), Beatrix, and sometimes Ivy; and a male one that would include Chinese, Dowager, Henry, and some other boys. I saw Dowager as mediating between the two little worlds, but also perhaps Ivy as doing so. And it's Ivy who was, unknowingly, to destroy this more or less utopian scene. Maybe it's obvious now what is "the matter" with Ivy — now in the 1990s when, rather oddly, it has happened that in so many contexts (therapy and fiction among them) narrative itself seems to have become coextensive with one particular narrative, that of childhood sexual abuse and its uncovery. That hadn't happened yet when I began imagining Ivy; from the beginning it was to have required a lot of interpretive work of new kinds with (among other things) Beatrix's photos, to so much as sow the suggestion of Ivy's having been molested over a fairly long period by Gene Protheroe. By the time she struggles to articulacy about these past events, the raffish, interpenetrating London households will have been established — only, as I finally imagined, to crash and burn in a big public scandal sparked by her accusations. Not that she would have accusations to level at anyone in either of the antifamily households, that is, but it seems almost inevitable that incipient scandal involving a *pere de famille* would get publicly articulated, instead, as a destructive panic about the more unconventional ménages in the vicinity. Asking myself how I had in mind to manage the radical metamorphosis of a clownishly stereotyped Humby into an (I hoped) dramatically dignified, highly individualized Dowager Jones, I look back at Trollope's letter to George Eliot in ch. 7, which tells (in however degraded form) the story of Humby's confusion on reading *The Mill on the Floss* back to back with *The Lifted Veil* under the impression he was still reading the same book. (Need I say that this actually happened to a friend of mine — not a semiliterate rustic, either; a Kant scholar!) It isn't a story about confusion, actually, so much as about the intense creativity that passionate readers seem willing to invest in preserving, and if necessary inventing, the continuity of the nexus of individual identity. One of the defining impulses of *The Warm Decembers* was to find new ways of trying, experimenting with, and honoring this form of creativity—when not more simply presuming on it. Ivy's "almost exactly the same dog" joke represents a version of it; in fact I see the whole poem as gathering instances of just such ontological thresholds and of the perverse, desiring energies that alone can move across them: between a person alive and dead; a person and a photograph; a sister and a sister; a present and a past; a person child and adult; people with the same name; a happening and the dream of it; a writer (or a model) and a character; an I and a she or he. (One way to describe the poem's first person is as an attempt to make the difference between I and she or he no *more* weighty or unappealable than these other differentials.)

In fact, this motive is the only sense I find I can make anymore of the image that was the unrealized germ of the poem. *The Warm Decembers* crystallized first around a scene that never got written. I was dancing in a disco in Ithaca (this would have been around 1978). My head was full of some foxhunting lore I'd just heard from an Irish critic, a hunting man himself. It was all new to me, or all of it I hadn't gathered from Trollope or Surtees: that hounds come in pairs, for instance, and are alphabetically named. Given the initial letter, the names will be "—oh, random *words*. The two might be named just anything. Charmer and Captivity, for instance." Now there's a random pair of words for you! The idea that came to me dancing was this: a long Victorian narrative poem that would include both a man named Miles and a hound named Miles. The hound Miles would be epileptic. At the formal climax of the poem the hound Miles would have a seizure, in the course of which he and the man Miles would somehow get their narrative points-of-view inextricably fused.

As the poem eventuated, something like this was probably going to happen—now between Trollope (revolving *Uncle Miles* in his mind) and the hound Miles. I suppose the bond that fuses them will have to do with each of their ability to experience landscape as narrative: the hound along the linear path of his sense of smell; Trollope through his addiction to interleaving with the rides of Sussex, the rides of Barsetshire. I can't remember, though, what was to have happened in or through this spectacular point-of-view effect. Maybe it was one of those spots, and there were a lot of them, that my mind had billboarded (like the billboards for rent that invite you to picture "YOUR MESSAGE HERE!") "your *tour de force* here!"

How happily I could go on pointing out the beauties of the poem's unwritten moiety. There's a sheaf of pages of widowed lines, reflections, incidents, jokes, epithets now placeless and near pointless. "'Do I take up any space in your life?'" "At every heartbeat, one pupil dilating, the other contracting." Of Mrs. Hatched,

> How many men were there who, dreaming of the scar,
> thought it was the cheek they were in love with?

Goatey's mental flight toward "the lares, penes, nates of his school." Beatrix and "the body's counterspeech." "What ties Beatrix's person, her art, Dowager, the poem's narrative together: firmness of enunciation with modesty of gaze. 'The cheerfully *averti*.'" "The girlish and the faux-girlish and . . . ?" "Re: Julia Margaret Cameron. Sticking the housemaid or neighbor into idyll, like sticking friends into WarmDecs. Lots about this?" "Living with books—either inside and lost in them or outside and lost to them."

> Trollope, next morning under pressure of
> Ellen's reflective singsong through his dream,
> her tiny orthodoxies, drop by drop
> of feminizing chilly lymph in his bladder
> —wakes early, tries his painful arm,
> adjusts with it the enormous truss,
> acidly touches at the exacerbated outline
> of a heroine who has (he sees)
> some tendency to shrink both from and in the wash.
>
> Through his high window comes no aiding image
> in the project of desiring.
> In rimey ruts where a wet month ago
> withdrawing carts embossed them, sour acorns freeze; demure,

demur, the words he likes for her endure
solstitial diminution, in his mouth.

"The char-à-banc to hushabye." "The oneiric disease": for me, they all resonate.

Sooner or later, I suppose, I will have to figure out why the remainder proved unable to be written. Certainly I hadn't (haven't) lost my love for the poem—nor at all my faith in the interest of its form. The most Victorian, the most novelistic thing about *The Warm Decembers* is the extreme heterogeneity of the ambitions that propelled it; which meant, too, that to fail it was to make many different failures. Loss of the poem was abrupt in the sense that, looking back, I can see that quite precisely the 1984 line "I see it in the body of Beatrix in the bath," in the middle of ch. 8, was the last one destined to have been written out of a relatively seamless sense of the integrity and momentum of this writing process. Yet it took me three or four more years of a punishing incredulity to understand that this poem was not being written. In fact, it was nine years from the time I left Beatrix in the bath before I seemed to be able to write poetry of any kind. The unyieldingness of these invisible brick walls!

I come up with a lot of kinds of attempts at explanation. Something heavy, intrapsychically, seems to have been going on in or around ch. 8—though looking back at my life and other writing of the time, I don't see its traces so clearly elsewhere. (But it seems relevant how much the poem is already about the underexplored terrain between a "depressiveness" that it attempts to celebrate and fructify, and a *depression* that always threatens the imaginative space thereby claimed.) Then, I suppose the poem must have been headed toward some kind of a plot crunch. So much of my resource and pleasure in the poem so far seem to come from the freedom to introduce new characters and plot elements ad libitum; perhaps it was inevitable that at some moment the narrative must have turned insupportably from an open into a closed system. I do carry on in the poem (and always conceived new ambitions for it) as extravagantly as if I had no sense of any limits to my powers of narrative writing, furthermore; but to be as steeped as this poem and its author were in the high realist manner was also to feel acutely the bite of every lacking skill. Also the ecology of genres was changing around *The Warm Decembers*. Part of my motive as a poet was that the most writerly writing I could do, and the most thinkerly thinking, be shown not to be generically alien to each other. But literary critics, I among them, were meanwhile beginning at the other end too, experimenting with increasingly elastic understandings of what kinds of writing the genre of criticism might accommodate. And the sense of there being a coherent, engaged, demanding and changing, highly queer, and highly inter-locutory audience of peers for ambitious critical writing—especially with the emergence of gay studies—marked an almost indescribable difference from the exiguous relations surrounding a young poet at the same moment.

Looking back, though, I feel it anew—in how many ways even the thinkiest narrative poem is a stranger to even the most writerly criticism. Ontological thresholds not to be denied or dissolved, but sought out with longing; where possible crossed and recrossed, even at the risks of estrangement, loss, deformation, abandonment. How should I even pretend to promise never to try it again?

Eve Kosofsky Sedgwick is the Newman Ivey White
Professor of English Literature at Duke University.
She is the author of *Tendencies,*
Epistemology of the Closet and *Between Men:*
English Literature and Male Homosocial Desire
and is an editor of Series Q.

Library of Congress Cataloging-in-
Publication Data
Sedgwick, Eve Kosofsky.
Fat art, thin art / Eve Kosofsky Sedgwick.
ISBN 0-8223-1501-7. —ISBN 0-8223-1512-2 (pbk.)
I. Title. PS3569.E316F37 1994
811'.54—dc20   94-8787 CIP